The World is Flat?

Also from
Meghan-Kiffer Press

EXTREME COMPETITION:
INNOVATION AND THE GREAT 21ST CENTURY
BUSINESS REFORMATION

MORE FOR LESS:
THE POWER OF PROCESS MANAGEMENT

BUSINESS PROCESS MANAGEMENT:
THE THIRD WAVE

IT DOESN'T MATTER:
BUSINESS PROCESSES DO

THE REAL-TIME ENTERPRISE:
COMPETING ON TIME

THE DEATH OF 'E' AND
THE BIRTH OF THE REAL NEW ECONOMY

Acclaim for our books:

Featured book recommendation
Harvard Business School's *Working Knowledge*

Book of the Year—*Internet World*

Meghan-Kiffer Press
Tampa, Florida, USA
www.mkpress.com
Innovation at the Intersection of Business and Technology

What Friedman's Critics are Saying

"Ultimately, Friedman's work is little more than advertising. The goal is not to sell the high-tech gadgetry described in page after page of the book, but to sell a way of life—a world view glorifying corporate capitalism and mass consumption as the only paths to progress. It is a view intolerant of lives lived outside the global marketplace. It betrays [unconsciously reveals] a disregard for democracy and a profound lack of imagination. This book's lighthearted style might be amusing were it not for the fact that his subject—the global economy—is a matter of life and death for millions. Friedman's words and opinions, ill informed as they are, shape the policies of leaders around the world. Many consider him to be a sophisticated thinker and analyst—not a propagandist. *It is a sobering reminder of the intellectual paralysis gripping our society today.*"
—**Roberto J. Gonzalez, Professor of Anthropology, San Jose State University**

"With all due respect to Tom Friedman, there's nothing flat about this unbalanced global economy. Clearly, the Chinese producer on the supply side and the American consumer on the demand side are the two major engines of the world economy. In a flat world, these two engines would be working together in near perfect harmony. In today's world, however, they are like passing ships in the night—cruising full speed ahead on their own journeys in increasingly choppy seas. Globalization at this point in time is far more about disparities between nations than the assimilation of a flat world."
—**Steven Roach, Chief Economist, Morgan Stanley**

"In the field of international affairs one of America's most prominent popularisers is Thomas Friedman, the leading columnist on the subject for the *New York Times*. He has won three Pulitzer prizes. If anyone should be able to explain the many complicated political, economic and social issues connected to the phenomenon of globalisation, it should be him. What a surprise, then, that his latest book is such a dreary failure.

"Mr. Friedman's book is subtitled 'A Brief History of the Twenty-First Century,' but it is not brief, it is not any recognisable form of history—except perhaps of Mr. Friedman's own wanderings around the world—and the reference to our new, baby century is just gratuitous. Even according to Mr. Friedman's own account, the world has been globalising since 1492. This kind of imprecision—less kind readers might even use the word 'sloppiness'—permeates Mr. Friedman's book. Mr. Friedman portrays himself as a modern-day Columbus. Of course, the entrepreneur [who triggered his 'flat world' metaphor], even by Mr. Friedman's own account, said nothing of the kind. But Mr. Friedman has discovered his metaphor for globalisation, and now nothing will stop him. He shows his readers no mercy, proceeding to flog this inaccurate and empty image to death over hundreds of pages.

"In his effort to prove that the world is flat (he means 'smaller'), Mr. Friedman talks to many people and he quotes at length lots of articles by other writers, as well as e-mails, official reports, advertising jingles, speeches and statistics. His book contains a mass of information. Some of it is relevant to globalisation. Like many journalists, he is an inveterate name-dropper, but he does also manage to interview some interesting and knowledgeable people. Mr. Friedman's problem is not a lack of detail. It is that he has so little to say. Over and over again he makes the same few familiar points: the world is getting smaller, this process seems inexorable, many things are changing, and we should not fear this. Rarely has so much information been collected to so little effect."

— **"Confusing Columbus,"** *The Economist*

"'In a flat world,' Friedman writes, 'you can innovate without having to emigrate.' Friedman is not alone in this belief: for the better part of the past century economists have been writing about the leveling effects of technology. From the invention of the telephone, the automobile, and the airplane to the rise of the personal computer and the Internet, technological progress has steadily eroded the economic importance of geographic place—or so the argument goes. By almost any measure the international economic landscape is not at all flat. On the contrary, our world is amazingly "spiky." In terms of both sheer economic horsepower and cutting-edge innovation, surprisingly few regions truly matter in today's global economy. What's more, the tallest peaks—the cities and regions that drive the world economy—are growing ever higher, while the valleys mostly languish."

—**Richard Florida, "The World is Spiky,"** *Atlantic Monthly*

"Friedman's image of a flat earth is profoundly misleading—a view of the world from a seat in business class. Flatness is another way of describing the transnational search by companies for cheap labor, an image that misses the pervasiveness of global inequality and the fact that much of the developing world remains mired in poverty and misery. It also misses the importance of the global geopolitical hierarchy, which guarantees the provision of stability, property rights, and other international public goods. The rise of China and India is less about flatness than it is about dramatic upheavals in the mountains and valleys of the global geopolitical map."

—**G. John Ikenberry,** *Foreign Affairs.*

"Thesis: Clearly, it is now possible for more people than ever to collaborate and compete in real time with more other people on more different kinds of work from more different corners of the planet and on a more equal footing than at any previous time in the history of the world – using computers, email, networks, teleconferencing, and dynamic new software." Source: A

social studies paper from a middling high school student, or a scintillating study from the *New York Times'* most prominent columnist? In its sloppy jalopy cadence and stunning banality, this sentence suggests a tenth-grader's efforts. But to Thomas Friedman's embarrassment, this statement fuels his car-wreck of a new book, *The World Is Flat*.... This nearly 500-page tome [600 for the 2nd edition] is a testament to our age along the lines of London's Millennium Dome—a monstrosity of poor design, cloudy thinking, and rank hubris. Oh well, Friedman is laughing all the way to the bank as he has another best-seller. In terms of substance, style, and significance, the only competitor [for *The World is Flat*] will be Donald Trump's hair."
—Randy Boyagoda, Books Editor, the *Weekly Standard*

"*The World Is Flat* is no more a study of global economics than *Batman Begins* is a social-policy treatise. It juggles a similar conundrum: how to present the wealthiest overlord of Gotham as a beneficent force in a world where generalized immiseration is caused not by staggering concentrations of wealth but by, y'know, gangsters [Al-Qaeda]. Friedman's flatness—wherein capitalism, having overcome any countervailing forces, fulfills the promises of progress—is Francis Fukuyama's *End of History*,' translated into the language of irrational exuberance. 'And now the icing on the cake,' the book moons, 'the übersteroid that makes it all mobile: wireless. Wireless is what will allow you to take everything that has been digitized, made virtual and personal, and do it from anywhere.' Leapin' übersteroids."
—Johsua Clover, *Village Voice*

"Thomas Friedman earns plaudits for his column which today announces that East Indians are taking jobs the French are too lazy to do ['A Race to the Top,' *New York Times*]. His fit of racial profiling was motivated by his pique over France's rejection of the globalizers' charter for corporate dominance known as the European Constitution. It's not the implicit racism of Friedman's statement which is most irksome, it's his ghastly glee that 'a world of benefits they [Western Europeans] have known for 50 years is coming apart,' because the French and other Europeans 'are trying to preserve a 35-hour work week in a world where Indian engineers are ready to work a 35-hour day.' He forgot to add, 'and where Indian families are ready to sell their children into sexual slavery to survive.' Now, THERE'S a standard to reach for.

"What Friedman means is that the French should give up their taste for old age pensions, universal health care, top-quality public education, protection of their skies and waters and all those things we used to call advances but now, according to the Friedman world order, stand in the way of progress. It is too bad that the Times' opinion columns have not been outsourced to India. Were it so, a Keralite might explain to Friedman that human advances are measured not by our willingness to crawl lower and lower to buy ourselves a job from Bill Gates, or by counting the number of Gap

outlets in Delhi, but by our success in protecting and nurturing liberté, égalité and fraternité among all humanity."
—Greg Palast, "French Fried Friedman."

"The blurb points in a wholly different direction: '... the convergence of technology and events that allowed India, China, and so many other countries to become part of the global supply chain for services and manufacturing, creating an explosion of wealth in the middle classes of the world's two biggest nations and giving them a huge new stake in the success of globalization? And with this "flattening" of the globe, which requires us to run faster in order to stay in place, has the world gotten too small and too fast for human beings and their political systems to adjust in a stable manner?'

"Huh? That last sentence packs in at least two too many metaphors for me to process: a flat earth, people running faster but staying in place, a small world and a fast world. And then there is the 'explosion' in the previous sentence. What is Friedman getting at with this mélange of metaphors?

"Clearly there is a book to be written about the impacts of the dramatic decline in transportation and communication costs that we have recently experienced – cargo containerization, air shipment, telecommunications, the Internet, e-mail, voice-mail and the cell phone. The title of that book would not be *The World is Flat*. The title would be *It's a Small World After All*. Physically, culturally, and economically the world is not flat. Never has been, never will be. There may be vast flat plains inhabited by indistinguishable *hoi polloi* doing mundane tasks, but there will also be hills and mountains from which the favored will look down on the masses."
—Prof. Edward Leamer, UCLA School of Management

"By presenting open sourcing in the same category as outsourcing and off shore production, Friedman hides corporate greed, corporate monopolies and corporate power, and presents corporate globalisation as human creativity and freedom. This is deliberate dishonesty, not just result of flat vision. That is why in his stories from India he does not talk of Dr. Hamid of CIPLA who provided AIDS medicine to Africa for $ 200 when U.S. corporations wanted to sell them for $20,000 and who has called WTO's patent laws 'genocidal.' And in spite of Friedman's research team having fixed an appointment with me to fly down to Bangalore to talk about farmers' suicides for the documentary Friedman refers to, Friedman cancelled the appointment at the last minute.

"Telling a one sided story for a one sided interest seems to be Friedman's fate. That is why he talks of 550 million Indian youth overtaking Americans in a flat world. When the entire Information Technology and outsourcing sector in India employs only a million out of a 1.2 billion people. Food and farming, textiles and clothing, health and education are nowhere in Friedman's monoculture of mind locked into IT.

"Friedman presents a 0.1% picture and hides 99.9%. And in the 99.9%

are Monsanto's seed monopolies and the suicides of thousands of farmers. In the eclipsed 99.9% are the 25 million women who disappeared in high growth areas of India because a commodified world has rendered women a dispensable sex. In the hidden 99.9% economy are thousands of tribal children in Orissa, Maharashtra, Rajasthan who died of hunger because the public distribution system for food has been dismantled to create markets for agribusiness. The world of the 99.9% has grown poorer because of the economic globalisation. Free-trade is about corporate freedom and citizen disenfranchisement. What Friedman is presenting as a new 'flatness' is in fact a new caste system, a new Brahminism, locked in hierarchies of exclusion."

—Dr. Vandana Shiva,
The Foundation for Science, Technology & Ecology

"Moving swiftly on to a subject of altogether more substantial significance, namely the hygiene habits of famous hacks, we are mildly intrigued to learn from Greg Palast ('the most impressive investigative reporter of our time') that when on the road, *New York Times* star columnist and Pulitzer Prize-winning commentator Thomas Friedman 'has a clean pair of underpants Fed-Exed to him every day, and puts the dirty ones in a return envelope.' If this important story is in the remotest degree true, we can but salute him."

—John Henley, *The Guardian*

"Friedman is impregnably armed by his good intentions and his ignorance. In *The World Is Flat* Friedman has produced an epyllion to the glories of globalisation with only three flaws: the writing style is prolix, the author is monumentally self-obsessed, and its content has the depth of a puddle. Throughout the book the metaphor of a flat Earth is reproduced again and again. What was not a particularly useful image to begin with is flogged to death until only the bones remain. At the same time, Friedman's laptop may need the 'I' key replaced, such is the hammering it must have absorbed from the author's use of the personal pronoun. In the course of the book we learn much—too much—about Friedman's family, friends and eating habits, culminating in a paean to his school journalism teacher ('I sit up straight just thinking about her!')."

—Richard Adams, *The Guardian*

"'When did you first realise that the world had become flat?' The *New York Times'* star columnist Thomas Friedman has asked that question of people in many different countries, and scatters their answers throughout his new book. But [readers] may also find themselves posing the question that I began to ask myself: 'When did you first realise that this book had become irritating?' Was it, for example, when I got tired of Friedman's attempts to tie up every point he makes in a catchy metaphor? (Success in modern business requires being not 'the vanilla ice cream' but 'the chocolate sauce and

the cherry on the top.') Was it when he adopted the tone of those inspirational how-to books that are sold in airport bookshops? ('Rule #1: When the world goes flat - and you are feeling flattened - reach for a shovel and dig inside yourself.') Was it when I noticed the repeated paragraphs and the ill-written sentences? Was it the relentlessly folksy tone that wore me down? ('The math/science salmon that swims upstream in China and gets hired by a foreign company is one smart fish'; 'Holy cow!'; 'Holy catfish!'; 'Boy!'; 'Wow!')"
—Noel Malcolm, *Daily Telegraph*

"This is a dangerous book, in a sense that it serves to make the average reader believe his 'hypotheses' about globalization (they aren't theories). Globalization is not a neutral phenomenon and as appealing as the 'Dell theory'[of conflict prevention] [Chapter 14] sounds, it excludes so many elements and actors that it could be turned around and be called the banana theory: there is not one country that exports bananas in which people are not exploited. What a sad story for someone who works for one of the top newspapers of the developed world."
—Michel Tremblay, Reviewer at Amazon.co.uk

"There are some truths in *The World Is Flat*, as there will be in most good propaganda, but the truths he leaves out (and that wealthier people sometimes avoid, consciously or not) make books like this a big lie. The 'anti-globalization' crowd that Friedman derides actually understands quite a bit about the misery caused by economic machinations, which crusaders of neoliberalism/Reaganomics don't chat about during their fancy cocktail parties. Critics of the new feudalism tend not to be 'anti-globalization' but rather anti-corporate tyranny."
—Preston Enright, Reviewer at Amazon.com

"Ok. The world is flat. That gets stated in first few pages. Then it gets repeated. Over and over and over. Bored? Skip to the middle and read 10 pages. Skip back a few chapters and read 10 more. Skip to the back and read the last 10. Then back somewhere and read another 10. You can do this repeatedly and not lose any continuity. Makes no difference."
—Dukes Sheep, Reviewer at Amazon.com

"Friedman is not an economist and honestly, his attempts at a foray into this field are as insulting as a 2 year old's finger paintings being sold as a Van Gogh. ...it's good from far, but far from good and completely devoid of the depth and articulation necessary to be considered anything other than a fraud."
—Jennifer M. Corby, Reviewer at Amazon.com

"The world is pretty darn flat when you're having lunch with CEOs at Five Star Hotels. And the world may be quite flat from here to the Bangalore office but outside of the Bangalore office the drop off is very steep indeed. The world is only flat for the tiny percentage of college graduates in India and China—the rest of the vast population lives in the garbage of that tiny majority. Globalization has not made and will not make any significant dent on the lives of these people, but Friedman, of course, didn't have lunch with any of them."
—J. Gunning, Reviewer at Amazon.com

"I believe, Friedman is well intentioned, but he mistakenly believes that he can find the truth through anecdotes. So, his empirical evidence comes from stories of things that he does not understand instead of the use of reliable demographic and economic databases. He believes that 10 exogenous forces can explain how 'the world became flat.' While doing this, he solely looks at the labor market and ignores the effects of the consumer, monetary, raw material/energy, and fixed investment markets. He cannot distinguish between a symptom and a cause. These 10 forces that he claims changed the labor markets are not causes but merely symptoms. Friedman is a name dropper par excellence, and rubs elbows with the elite. Unfortunately for him, he cannot detect competence or incompetence. The book is filled with inconsistency. It derides the inflexibility of the European welfare state, but calls for an American safety net to protect those from globalization. America's increasing indebtedness is not given one sentence in this book. Not only are jobs being exported to Southeast Asia, but claims and control on American assets are also being transferred. Increasingly, the important capital allocations in America will be directed by foreign executives who will be even less accountable than the Bernie Ebbers and the Ken Lays. In short, Friedman is not qualified to write on this topic, but like the incompetent overpaid executives that he hangs with, he will be over paid, and over read. At best, we might be able to profit if we understand how this 'conventional wisdom' is wrong and then short sell the companies whose leaders make bad decisions based on this wrong analysis."
—Ralph Bradley, Reviewer at Amazon.com

"This is a terrible book that sends the exact wrong message: the world is 'flat,' so people are now equal and there are no inequities to address. At a time when the world is becoming less and less flat every day, as the rich get richer and the poor get poorer, Friedman's book unfortunately pulls a great curtain over the eyes of the American people and sends our pop punditry down further into an even deeper state of shame."
—T. Wu, Reviewer at Amazon.com

"Clearly Friedman's vision of a flat earth won't come true until we solve the paradox of how to make humans into a race of mindless, overachieving, underpaid automatons who still somehow manage to think creatively enough to constantly invent enough new technology to create new jobs at the same rate as the old jobs are being outsourced."
—P. Peterson, Reviewer at Amazon.com

"Simplistic anecdotes that condescend to the reader. Friedman fails to live up to his own conceptual assertions, time and time again. A waste of time, and dangerous because Friedman writes in a way that people FEEL like he's distilled the issues in a way that's utterly understandable; instead, he's left out 80% of any given issue."
—Melvin G. Brennan III, Amazon Reviewer from Scotland

"Thomas Friedman's work reminds me of PT Barnum. I am an economics student in the United States and London and also work for an NGO working on environmental issues and poverty. He pulls off his black magic because so many of us exist in full ignorance of what conditions for the poor are really like or how markets really work. I beg you. Please read some authors who are critical of neo-liberalism and Friedman in particular."
—Juniper Rose, Reviewer at Amazon.com

The World is Flat?

A Critical Analysis of the New York Times Bestseller by Thomas Friedman

Ronald Aronica
Mtetwa Ramdoo

Meghan-Kiffer Press
Tampa, Florida, USA
www.mkpress.com
Innovation at the Intersection of Business and Technology

Publisher's Cataloging-in-Publication Data

Aronica, Ronald.
    The World is Flat? : A Critical Analysis of the New York Times
    Bestseller by Thomas Friedman / Ronald Aronica, Mtetwa Ramdoo - 1st ed.
    p. cm.
    Includes index.
    ISBN-10: 0-929652-04-5 (alk. paper)
    ISBN-13: 978-0-929652-04-7 (alk. paper)

    1. Diffusion of innovations. 2. Information Society. 3. Globalization—Social
aspects. 4. Globalization—Economic aspects. I. Aronica, Ronald. II. Ramdoo,
Mtetwa. III. Title.

HM486.A75 2006   2006931068
303.48'33–dc22   CIP

Published by Meghan-Kiffer Press
310 East Fern Street — Suite G
Tampa, FL 33604 USA

Company and product names mentioned herein are the trademarks or registered
trademarks of their respective owners.

Meghan-Kiffer books are available at special quantity discounts for corporate education and training use. For more information write Special Sales, Meghan-Kiffer
Press, Suite G, 310 East Fern Street, Tampa, Florida 33604 or email
info@mkpress.com

Meghan-Kiffer Press
Tampa, Florida, USA
www.mkpress.com
Innovation at the Intersection of Business and Technology

Printed in the United States of America.   SAN 249-7980
MK Printing 10 9 8 7 6 5 4 3 2 1

This book is dedicated to those who want to go beyond the media hype and the metaphors to more fully understand the global forces shaping the twenty-first century—for globalization is the greatest reorganization of the world since the Industrial Revolution.

Why this book?

Thomas Friedman's book, *The World is Flat,* is a dangerous book. It treats *the* issue of our time, globalization, from a restricted and superficial perspective.

Yet, the book has been a hands-down bestseller for two years and counting. The notion of globalization has been around for centuries, and has taken many forms: political, economic, cultural, and technological, to name a few. But the twenty-first century-style globalization that Friedman writes about is unique. It has a name: "corporate" globalization.

Today, leading economists, both advocates and critics of globalization, agree that international trade has improved the lives of many across the world, bringing technology and knowledge to virtually every corner of the globe, and has raised many above the tyranny of backward and often repressive cultures. This book and its critical analysis agrees with this assessment but points out that which is left out in Friedman's paean to corporate globalization. It is *what gets left out* that makes Friedman's book so dangerous.

In the 1980s, capitalism triumphed over communism. By the year 2050, communist China is expected to have a gross domestic product (GDP) twice that of the United States.

Who triumphed?

That's something to think about, and what we want this book to do is to go beyond Friedman's superficial treatment of globalization and encourage readers who were awed by his book to "think again." We hope you learn much form this little book, and enjoy some of the bits of parody.

Ronald Aronica
Mtetwa Ramdoo
August 2006

Contents

Globalization: <u>The</u> Issue of Our Times

Globalization is the greatest reorganization of the world since the Industrial Revolution. Unfortunately, there is no universally understood definition of globalization. Most ideas about globalization focus on different aspects of the growing interdependence at economic, cultural and technological levels. In short, the world is being interconnected more and in many more ways. Some even speak of a unified "global society," a melting pot for all the world's societies. "Homogenization via the Internet." "The End of History." "The Triumph of Democratic Capitalism." And, more recently, "A Flat World."

But not so fast.

Globalization is a highly complex interaction of forces. Not only does it exhibit integration, it also exhibits disintegration.

It is rooted in cooperation—and it is rooted in violence.

For some, it represents the triumph of free-market capitalism over communism, ushering in democracy, world peace and universal prosperity—for others, it represents conflict, unbridled greed, deregulated corporate power, and an utter disregard for humanity.

Yet, the person on the street, especially in America, has little clue what globalization is all about. Few have any doubt that change is placing the world under great stress, that it is being turned upside down. And they may suspect that it has to do with the word, which increasingly appears in the press and other media: globalization. But what does it really mean? It would be great if a popularizer, a famous personality or pundit, would explain the many complicated political, economic and social issues connected to the phenomenon of globalization.

Desperate for such information, millions of people, including leaders in government and education, have turned to Thomas Friedman's mass market book, *The World is Flat,* to gain an understanding of globalization. Unfortunately, they are served up stories from friends, elite CEOs and other personal contacts of the author.

On Bullshit

Before we begin to analyze Friedman's book, let's spend a few moments reflecting on what Professor Harry G. Frankfurt wrote in his book, *On Bullshit,* (Princeton University Press, 2005). "Both in lying and in telling the truth people are guided by their beliefs concerning the way things are. These guide them as they endeavor either to describe the world correctly or to describe it deceitfully. For this reason, telling lies does not tend to unfit a person for telling the truth in the same way that bullshitting tends to. Through excessive indulgence in the latter activity, which involves making assertions without paying attention to anything except what it suits one to say, a person's normal habit of attending to the ways things are may become attenuated or lost. Someone who lies and someone who tells the truth are playing on opposite sides, so to speak, in the same game. Each responds to the facts as he understands them, although the response of the one is guided by the authority of the truth, while the response of the other defies that authority and refuses to meet its demands. The bullshitter ignores these demands altogether. He does not reject the authority of the truth, as the liar does, and oppose himself to it. He pays no attention to it at all."

Professor Frankfurt argues that bullshitters misrepresent themselves to their audience not as liars do, that is, by deliberately making false claims about what is true. In fact, bullshit need not be untrue at all.

Rather, bullshitters seek to convey a certain impression of themselves without being concerned about whether anything at all is true. They quietly change the rules governing their end of the conversation so that claims about truth and falsity are irrelevant. Frankfurt concludes that, although bullshit can take many innocent forms, excessive indulgence in it can eventually undermine the practitioner's capacity to tell the truth in a way that lying does not. Liars at least acknowledge that it matters what is true. "By virtue of this," Frankfurt writes, "bullshit is a greater enemy of the truth than lies are."

Because the world is undergoing the greatest reorganization since the beginning of the Industrial Revolution, a rigorous and complete analysis is needed to guide our leaders and us in the brave new world of total global competition. Unfortunately, in a small book such as this, we are only able to scratch the surface and provide you, the reader, with a counterbalance to Friedman's rosy picture of globalization and its effects. To help readers get a fuller understanding of the issues, we provide suggested readings at the end of this book. Sure, it may take more effort to read more rigorous discussions of globalization, especially if these discussions aren't based almost totally on personal anecdotes, and stories spun from meeting one's daughter's friend's boyfriend at Yale, or playing golf with rich and famous corporate executives. While readers probably cannot find a single lie in Friedman's book, neither can they find the whole truth, nor most of the important facets of globalization.

While Friedman's personal anecdotes fascinate many readers and make for good tales at cocktail parties, it's what's left out of story after story after story that makes the book such a flawed distillation of globalization. Thus, it is what's ignored on the many issues that Friedman touches upon that makes the book dangerous, for it gives average readers a false sense that they are gaining a true understanding of this broad and complex subject.

In this day of consolidated big media pushing its high-profile authors, Friedman surely is a pundit who has a real money tree in his tabloid-style book on globalization. The problem is that the book has the potential to do great harm. But, before we take his book to task with any sort of critical analysis, let's first explore some of the praise it has received.

One of the world's leading thinkers: Thomas Friedman?

"At the beautiful Savannah International Trade and Convention Center on Friday, March 31, 2006, with the sun glinting off the Savannah River nearby, two of the world's leading thinkers—Thomas Friedman (*The World is Flat*) and former President Bill Clinton—joined the many speakers at the two-day (March 31 and April 1) Inc. 500 conference, which celebrates the achievements of the men and women who have created the 500 fastest-growing private companies in America. For many in the Georgia technology industry, Friedman's book has become a treasured guide through the jungle of the 21st century—steering them through the rapid changes which have shaken the world since the new millennium dawned."

— www.thecreativecoast.org

While The Creative Coast Initiative anoints Friedman as one of the world's leading thinkers, that organization is not alone. Just read the praise from his own newspaper, *The New York Times*, "The metaphor of a flat world, used by Friedman to describe the next phase of globalization, is ingenious. It came to him after hearing an Indian software executive explain how the world's economic playing field was being leveled. For a variety of reasons, what economists call 'barriers to entry' are being destroyed; today an individual or company anywhere can collaborate or compete globally. Bill Gates explains the meaning of this transformation best. Thirty years ago, he tells Friedman, if you had to choose between being born a genius in Mumbai or Shanghai and an average person in Poughkeepsie, you would have chosen Poughkeepsie because your chances of living a prosperous and fulfilled life were much greater there. 'Now,' Gates says, 'I would rather be a genius born in China than an average guy born in Poughkeepsie.'" [1]

Then read what one reviewer wrote in the *Boston Globe*, "Thomas L. Friedman, three-time winner of the Pulitzer Prize and foreign affairs columnist for *The New York Times*, offers a tantalizing look at the future in *The World Is Flat*. He writes: 'Here's the truth that no one wanted to tell you. The world has been flattened. As a result [commerce has] been made cheaper, easier, more friction-free, and more productive for more people from more corners of the earth than at any time in the history of the world.'"[2]

And the *Christian Science Monitor* reports, "This book is really a manual, or an idiot's guide to surviving in the computer age. It provides specific steps for individuals, companies, and poor nations to adapt to a 'flat world.' Friedman's advice to his own daughters: 'Girls, finish your homework—people in China and India are starving for your jobs.'

"But he also gives advice to leaders on such policies as free trade and how to help that half of humanity which still lives in the unflat world. He warns that those not plugged into new technologies can actually do harm, because in a flat world, 'if you don't visit a bad neighborhood, it might visit you.' He wants business and government to show more imagination in using and expanding this new world.

"No one today chronicles global shifts in simple and practical terms quite like Friedman. He plucks insights from his travels and the published press that can leave you spinning like a top."

And, from the *Spectator*, "The masters of business writing are not generally touched by the poet's sensibility. It is hardly surprising that delicate souls adopt a pained expression when confronted with the serried ranks of macho titles like Revival of the Fittest or Getting to Yes. Frankly, the heart scarcely leaps at a book that puts 'The Globalized World' in the subtitle to *The World is Flat*. This is all very unfortunate because *The World is Flat's* author, Thomas Friedman, although not the most subtle of literary stylists, is one of a small number of communicators who writes intelligibly about trends in international economics."[3]

And, across the pond in the U.K., the *Telegraph* had this to say,

"Thomas Friedman has been called 'the most important columnist in America today' by the *New York Times*. The glory is only slightly diminished by the realisation that it's the *New York Times* for which he is a columnist. He is best known as a prophet of (his detractors would say, a cheerleader for) globalisation, having come to prominence through his book *The Lexus and the Olive Tree* (1999), in which he argued that the new mobility of ideas and capital (represented by the Lexus) could strengthen, rather than threaten, local identities (the olive tree). Now, thanks to the collapse of trade barriers and the spread of information technology, work could follow the supply of labour."[4]

Let's now consider a more comprehensive review of Friedman's book.

The Pundit and the Money Tree

In "The Pundit and the Money Tree," Amitabh Pal, writes that "Friedman can't resist the impulse to be cutesy. Here he is explaining how cultural conservatives and labor are on one side in opposing globalization, with businessmen and the information industry on the other:

"'*The Passion of the Christ* audience will be in the same trench with the Teamsters and the AFL-CIO, while the Hollywood and Wall Street liberals and the You've Got Mail crowd will be in the same trench with the high-tech workers of Silicon Valley and the global service providers of Manhattan and San Francisco,' Friedman writes. 'It will be Mel Gibson and Jimmy Hoffa Jr. versus Bill Gates and Meg Ryan.'

"So infatuated is he with what he considers to be his cleverness that he employs absolutely horrendous metaphors of 'vanilla' (representing a regular job), 'chocolate sauce' (value-added job), and 'the cherry on top' (the ultimate value-added job) to describe occupations in the United States. And he doesn't stop there. 'In China today, Bill Gates is Britney Spears,' Friedman writes. 'In America today, Britney Spears is Britney Spears--and that is our problem.'

"His cheesy style gets in the way of his main point: Technological forces—such as the Internet and outsourcing—have altered the nature of the workplace so fundamentally that they have changed the world. This, Friedman argues, has affected everything ranging from the way you order burgers at drive ups (the orders are often taken at some remote location) to the way cartoon movies are made (teams in

Bangalore, India, are frequently doing the animation) to the way computers are fixed (UPS runs a repair facility for Toshiba).

"He says these technological innovations, combined with the almost universal adoption of free market economics, have leveled the playing field for developing countries—hence the odd title of the book. As a result, a few billion more people have entered into the global workforce, most significantly in India and China, creating enormous opportunities for them and significantly benefiting the world as a whole, Friedman contends. At the same time, this has created worrisome competition for American workers, since a lot of their jobs—in manufacturing and services—can be now shipped off to China or India.

"The problem is that Friedman takes this thesis and then overstates it so greatly and pounds it home so hard that by the end you're left wincing. For much of the book, he makes it seem that these technological transformations are affecting almost everyone around the world. To cover his behind, he has one chapter that he dedicates to the 'unflat world:' people not benefiting from these changes, such as in rural areas in many parts of the globe, because they are left out of the technological loop. But the tone of the rest of the book is that everyone needs to get with the program of free trade, capitalism, and technological innovation.

"Much of the book is dedicated to cataloging the business practices of corporations that have, according to Friedman, transformed the world. These entities include Wal-Mart, UPS, Yahoo, and Google, and Friedman's extensive interviews with their executives give the book the feel of a puff job.

"Friedman's geeky enthusiasm leads him to hail every technological innovation as the next best thing since the microchip. So when he doesn't get a desired seat on a Southwest Airlines flight because many passengers themselves have printed out their boarding passes and are allowed to get on the plane earlier, he has an epiphany. 'Friedman,' I said to myself, looking at this scene, 'you are so twentieth-century … You are so Globalization 2.0.' In Globalization 1.0 there was a ticket agent. In Globalization 2.0 the e-ticket machine replaced the ticket agent. In Globalization 3.0 you are your own ticket agent.'

"While Friedman cautions that the dangers of outsourcing should not be overstated, he repeatedly raises the specter of people's jobs being sent overseas unless the American education system is overhauled or workers reinvent themselves. To prove his point, he cites a

Forrester Research study that estimates that three million jobs will be sent abroad by 2015. But this translates into an annual loss of 300,000 jobs. Currently, there are 135 million jobs in the U.S. economy. So why is he making such a big deal out of this tiny fraction? And he exaggerates the importance of jobs being created in the developing world due to technological innovation, even as he admits that the high-tech sector employs just 0.2 percent of the workforce in India, his main example.

"The jury is still out on whether Friedman's beloved globalization will bring any relief to the world's deprived. 'Trying to sell trade policy as a high-powered way for helping the poor—you can't do it with intellectual honesty,' Gary Hufbauer, an economist with the pro-trade Institute for International Economics, recently told *The Wall Street Journal.*

"When it comes to India, Friedman's favorite, free market policies have failed to reduce poverty any faster than the state-oriented policies before them, according to independent estimates. The free market has done worse in some respects. The rate of improvement for key health indicators in India, such as life expectancy and infant mortality, slowed in the 1990s. This deceleration came about because of policies carried out as part of the neoliberal* agenda, such as freezing public health expenditures, removing price controls on essential drugs, and subsidizing private hospitals at the expense of public ones, according to an article in *The Hindu* newspaper by Professor Gita Sen of the Indian Institute of Management at Bangalore. Thousands of farmers have committed suicide in rural India in the past few years partly as a result of 'price uncertainty due to trade liberalization and rise in costs due to domestic liberalization,' according to a study quoted in *Economic and Political Weekly.*

"As for the United States, a country that Friedman proudly holds up as the role model for the world, Berkeley economist David Levine recently pointed out in *The New York Times* that 'being born poor in the U.S. gives you disadvantages unlike anything in Western Europe

---

* **Neoliberalism,** as a philosophy, holds that free markets, free trade, and the free flow of capital are the most efficient ways to produce the greatest social, political, and economic good. It argues for reduced taxation, reduced regulation, and minimal government involvement in the economy. This includes the privatization of health and retirement benefits, the dismantling of trade unions, and the general opening up of the economy to foreign competition. Detractors see it as a power grab by economic elites and a race to the bottom for the rest.

and Japan and Canada.' Plus, overall poverty is higher in the United States. The U.S. poverty figure (17.1 percent) for 2000, for instance, was significantly higher than for most European countries. France, Germany, and the United Kingdom had poverty rates of 7.0 percent, 9.8 percent, and 11.4 percent, respectively. Canada and Japan were lower than the United States, too, with a poverty rate of 10.3 percent and 15.3 percent, respectively.

"One problem with Friedman is the extremely narrow net of informants who feed him notions that reinforce his beliefs. Friedman's Indian corporate buddies keep on supplying him half-truths and distortions that he accepts as gospel because they fit into his worldview. And even when he has a sensible person as the source, such as Nobel-winning economist Amartya Sen, he fails to get the right information from him. So Friedman and his sources lay all of India's problems on the supposedly socialist policies it followed till 1991. But Sen has said elsewhere that the 'tendency to describe our past up to 1991 as some kind of left-wing Nehruvian socialism' is 'really a monstrous absurdity.' Friedman's analysis contains such errors throughout, making you wish that he had spoken with more people who know reality outside the corporate boardrooms and office parks in India, individuals like journalist Palagummi Sainath or development expert Jean Dreze, who has co-authored a number of books (with none other than Amartya Sen) on the mixed record of economic liberalization in India.

"Friedman completely ignores the problems created by the Indian call center industry, such as the imposition of fake Western identities and the harshness of constantly working at night. He talks to timid employees and industry flacks and comes to the conclusion that all is well. In Friedman's world, 'Indian call center operators adopt Western names of their own choosing.' And the night shift fits 'in very nicely with the Indian day,' as he told Terry Gross of Fresh Air. He would have had a much less one-sided evaluation if he had talked to people like Arjun Raina, a call center trainer and theater performer featured on 60 Minutes who has written a play, A Terrible Beauty Is Born, on the plight of call center workers.

"Similarly, Friedman extols the shifting of global manufacturing to China, even approving of the downward tug that China exhibits on global standards. China 'has created a process of competitive flattening, in which countries scramble to see who can give companies the best tax breaks, education incentives, and subsidies, on top of their cheap labor, to encourage off-shoring to their shores.' Though wages may be flattening, too, he evidently assumes that everyone will win out by moving from vanilla to chocolate sauce to the cherry on top.

"Friedman is so enamored with globalization and technology that he is unable to tackle the issue in all its complexity. He constantly touts the jobs that outsourcing is creating in the developing world, but he never once mentions that globalization is a package deal that comes with less attractive features. One such aspect was recently on display in India. In order to comply with World Trade Organization rules, the Indian parliament granted strong patent protections to medicines a few months ago, a step that will probably make lifesaving medications such as AIDS drugs unaffordable in the future not only in India but all over the developing world, since India has been a major exporter of generic drugs.

"Another troubling feature of globalization is the patenting of life forms and seeds, a highly controversial subject in developing countries, but an issue that Friedman ignores.

"Nor does Friedman discuss currency liberalization, which means yielding control of your currency to speculators, a phenomenon that has harmed millions of people in developing nations. This was one of the primary causes for the Asian economic crisis of the late 1990s that devastated a number of countries.

"Friedman also fails to grapple with two of the most prominent critiques of globalization in recent years—Joseph Stiglitz's *Globalization and Its Discontents* and George Soros on *Globalization*. Friedman doesn't even mention either author, a huge omission, given that Stiglitz has won the Nobel Prize for Economics and that Soros is, well, Soros.

"Friedman almost totally ignores South America. This is not just a coincidence, since the region—once heralded as the poster child of globalization—has fallen on hard times, and the people of that region have repeatedly rejected the neoliberal model in recent elections. The only Latin American country that merits more than a passing mention is Mexico, with Friedman offering a feeble conjecture about 'intangibles' being the reason the country hasn't prospered in spite of NAFTA and the push toward a free market model.

"One of the very few references to Argentina is in a typically silly and paternalistic passage, where he proposes that countries that fail to achieve the proper level of globalization form Developing Countries Anonymous, modeled on Alcoholics Anonymous:

"Countries would have to stand up at their first meeting and say,

'My name is Syria and I'm underdeveloped.' Or 'My name is Argentina and I'm underachieving. I have not lived up to my potential.'

"Given how half-baked his book is, Friedman is the one who is underachieving and not living up to his potential."[5]

Doubting Thomas

There are many things that the uninitiated reader may not get from plowing through story after story, mixed metaphor after mixed metaphor in Friedman's book. So, we'll provide some notes as we walk through the book's content.

But first, let us turn to professor of anthropology at San Jose State University, Roberto J. Gonzalez, who succinctly summarizes key concerns about Friedman's book, "Over the past 15 years, Thomas Friedman's writing has influenced presidents, policy-makers and captains of industry across the world. His *New York Times* columns reach millions of people daily, and he has established himself as a leading member of the American punditry.

"Yet Friedman's latest book, *The World Is Flat*, is culturally misinformed, historically inadequate and intellectually impoverished. It is also a runaway best-seller.

"The book's main point is that the world is 'flattening'— becoming more interconnected—as the result of the Internet, wireless technology, search engines and other innovations. Consequently, corporate capitalism has spread like wildfire to China, India and Russia, where factory workers, engineers and software programmers are paid a fraction of what their American counterparts are paid.

"Business reporters, labor activists, historians and anthropologists have reported these trends for more than a decade, but Friedman would have us believe that he single-handedly discovered the 'flat world.' In fact, without a trace of irony, he compares himself to Christopher Columbus embarking upon a global journey of exploration. To awe his readers, Friedman relies upon anecdotes and vignettes from recent trips. He breathlessly recounts visiting booming Asian cities that he portrays as landscapes littered with American logos from IBM, Goldman Sachs, Microsoft and Pizza Hut. In Bangalore (India) and Dalian (China), cheerful CEOs and young high-tech workers explain how wonderful corporate globalization has been for them. Friedman gushes about golf courses and skyscrapers built by U.S. companies around the world; he raves about handheld gadgets that send faxes, snap photos and play MP3 tunes; and he reminisces about sushi bars in Dubai and Bentonville (the Arkansas home of Wal-Mart).

"Not until the final chapters does he acknowledge that most Indians and Chinese still live in poverty. He never mentions that the gap between rich and poor in both India and China is widening. Nor does he dwell on the fact that many of the companies that have laid off thousands of Bay Area employees (Santa Clara County alone lost 231,000 jobs between 2000 and 2004) have replaced them with workers in Asia.

"In the second half of the book, Friedman ponders the implications of living in a 'flat world.' He argues that for the United States and developing countries, this is both a crisis and an opportunity. In order to succeed, the United States must produce greater numbers of specialized workers, including lawyers, accountants, brain surgeons and computer designers. Developing countries must dismantle trade barriers, privatize state industries, invite foreign companies and change their attitudes. And the 'unflat world' (here Friedman really means the 'Arab-Muslim world' and sub-Saharan Africa) must get over its feelings of frustration, insecurity and illness.

"Toward the end of the book Friedman acknowledges that most of the global population does not live in a 'flat world'—and that many have no desire to do so. To explain this, he resorts to a facile explanation: culture. He argues that cultures open to foreign ideas (he really means open to corporate capitalism and mass consumption) will blossom in the 21st century, while closed cultures will wither.

"Friedman's understanding of culture is simplistic and sloppy. He relies upon analogies rather than analysis, stereotypes rather than social science, and hearsay rather than history. For example, he muses upon what the world's regions would look like if they were neighborhoods:

'Latin America would be the fun part of town, the club district, where the workday doesn't begin until ten p.m. and everyone sleeps until midmorning.... The Arab street would be a dark alley where outsiders fear to tread, except for a few side streets.... Africa, sadly, is that part of town where the businesses are boarded up, life expectancy is declining, and the only new buildings are health-care clinics.'

"Friedman seems vexed by what he calls the 'backwardness' of Arab and Muslim cultures. He writes, 'For complicated cultural and historical reasons, many of them do not glocalize [absorb foreign ideas] well.' Approvingly, he refers to economist David Landes, who argues that in the Arab Muslim world, 'cultural attitudes have in many ways become a barrier to development.'

"This reveals a shocking ignorance of history. For seven centuries, Islam was the global civilization par excellence, and it enabled the development of many scientific, intellectual and artistic breakthroughs during that period.

"Nowhere is the European (and American) colonization and occupation of the Arab and Muslim worlds over the last 200 years mentioned as a possible explanation for anger and resentment directed against the United States and Europe. Nowhere is U.S. government support of brutal dictatorships in the Middle East (from the shah to the Saudi royal family) offered as a possible reason for opposition to Western hegemony posing as 'globalization' or a 'flat world.' In this book, history is bunk.

"Friedman doesn't appear to spend much time outside of golf courses, five-star restaurants, limousines and luxury hotels. His view of the world is consistent with dozens of elites he interviews on his global journey. The chief executive officers of Fortune 500 companies, Mexican ex-presidents, U.S. secretaries of state and military generals, Japanese financial consultants and Indian and Chinese ministers of trade inhabit Friedman's flat world. The voices of farmers, factory workers and street vendors are heard nowhere in the text, though many might tell a different story—of growing poverty, hunger and disease in the wake of World Bank, International Monetary Fund, and World Trade Organization policies.

"Ultimately, Friedman's work is little more than advertising. The goal is not to sell the high-tech gadgetry described in page after page of the book, but to sell a way of life—a world view glorifying corporate capitalism and mass consumption as the only paths to progress. It is a view intolerant of lives lived outside the global marketplace. It betrays [unconsciously reveals] a disregard for democracy and a profound lack of imagination."

"This book's lighthearted style might be amusing were it not for the fact that his subject—the global economy—is a matter of life and death for millions. Friedman's words and opinions, ill informed as they are, shape the policies of leaders around the world. Many consider him to be a sophisticated thinker and analyst—not a propagandist. It is a sobering reminder of the intellectual paralysis gripping our society today."

Let us now take a quick fly-over of the content of the book, drawing from brief snippets found in Wikipedia, to give the reader a basic idea of what Friedman writes about in each chapter. In so doing, we will also alert you to what just could be considered as Professor Frankfurt's "bullshit."

Part 1: How the World Became Flat

Chapter 1: While I Was Sleeping

Wikipedia: Friedman presents himself as someone who has been distracted by international crises since the attacks of September 11, 2001, and who is now catching up with the progress of globalization. He discovers that while he was "sleeping," the world has entered into a new phase of globalization, whose history he briefly characterizes as follows: The years 1492 to 1800 were "Globalization 1.0," which was driven by countries and muscles; the years 1800 to 2000 were "Globalization 2.0," which was driven by multinational companies and came in two parts, the first marked by "falling transportation costs," and the second by "falling telecommunication costs"; the years beginning in 2000, and forming the subject of this volume, are "Globalization 3.0," which will be marked by the empowerment of individuals. He describes visits to Bangalore, India and Dalian, China. The experience of JetBlue with homesourcing in Utah, the military in Iraq with technology, various headlines from the press in 2004, and blogging serve as examples of the "Completely new social, political, and business models" that are emerging.

While Friedman was sleeping, others were not. When it comes to his discussions of "technology advances" and their impact on business, it's like searching for a needle in a haystack to find anything original in his 600 pages of grandiloquent prose. Most of his observations and analyses were written previously by more qualified and rigorous writers before and during the dot-com era. Readers may want to read the following to get a more complete look at technology advances: *New Rules for the New Economy : 10 Radical Strategies for a Connected World*, Kevin Kelly, 1998; *The Digital Economy*, Don Tapscott, 1995; *Global Paradox*, John Nasibitt, 1994; and *Enterprise E-Commerce*, Peter Fingar, 2000.

Friedman's thesis regarding the outsourcing of knowledge work as the next big thing was concisely described while he was asleep back in 2001 in an *Internet World* article, "The Globalization of White Collar Work." In case you don't have the time to absorb Friedman's major thesis by reading almost 600 pages of rambling personal anecdotes, here it is condensed into 417 words:

"We are witnessing the greatest professional employment migration in history. We have now crossed the globalization threshold for knowledge-based work, and the implications for business strategies are enormous as companies unbundle and rebundle themselves into stateless, transnational enterprises.

"Especially in the current economic downturn, transnationals will seek out low-cost labor in every aspect of their operations as they search for both cost savings and quality improvements (73 million people work for multinational companies worldwide). Indeed, globalization is a very real phenomenon and is transforming the world economic system, including not just production and distribution, but all aspects of business. Globalization is the central organizing principle of the post-cold war world.

"It's common knowledge that much of the Redmond software that we all use is programmed in Bangalore. Software development is an obvious example of white collar globalization. Innovation becomes stateless and even the most creative, most esteemed jobs migrate to clusters of excellence around the globe (90% of Hollywood's animation production happens in Asia).

"The lesson here is that it's not the corporation's low-level, low-wage jobs nor the non–mission-critical activities that are being globalized. Finance and accounting services for GE Capital world wide are managed from India. Basic research is booming in Russia. Here are some indicators from India: American Express processes internal financial transactions for all of Asia and employs 600 people while the U.S. finance organization has shrunk by 60%; GE Capital employs 2,000 people managing global payroll, call centers, mortgage and insurance claims and is expected to have 8,000 by the end of 2003; and British Airways employs hundreds of people to handle an array of back office applications.

"Companies need not only extend business processes to their suppliers and customers, they must zero in on their internal core competencies, on the ways in which they add value as they unbundle and rebundle their organizations in the global economy. It won't be just the satellite/fiber hybrid networks that drive the continued globalization of highly skilled knowledge workers, it will be the ability to blend content and knowledge management, including e-learning, and extend it 'internally' across the globe. For better or worse, we have already crossed the threshold to the globalization of our most prized asset, the value-adding core competencies of our enterprise. Historians will measure the scale and impact of white collar globalization against the Industrial Revolution itself. You fat cats sitting in the plush administrative offices of American companies—beware. A fully qualified, $40k a year CxO in Durban has his eyes on your job."

_____*Internet World,* 2001

After Friedman wakes up, and just after comparing himself to Columbus, he gives us warning of the level of rigor that we can expect for the rest of the book, "Columbus reported to his king and queen that the world was round, and he went down in history as the man who first made this discovery [historically wrong]. I returned home [from India] and shared my discovery only with my wife, and only in a whisper. 'Honey,' I confided, 'I think the world is flat.'"

Which world? According to the University of Sheffield's Ankie Hoogvelt, "Just 28% of the world population lives in regions which attract 90% of all foreign direct investment flows."[6]

Perhaps a more accurate opening boast from Friedman should have been, "Honey, I really don't mean the world is flat, I just meant the exclusive golf course on which I am playing here in Bangalore. But, what the heck, with my *New York Times* platform, I think I can whip together a book of stories from the people I've met here in India, sell a few million copies. I'll tell everyone how all these young Zippies in India are now 'empowered individuals' ready to take over the world's economy, just like how the multinational corporations of Globalization 2.0 before them, grabbed power."

What's this stuff about Globalization 3.0 and "empowering the individual?"

Friedman famously quotes Bill Gates, "The kid who is connected to the Internet today, if he has the curiosity and an Internet connection, is as empowered as me."

Really? What kind of absurdity is that?

Robert Wright, a visiting fellow at Princeton University's Center for Human Values asks, 'What do you call it when multinational corporations scan the world for cheap labor, find poor people in developing nations, and pay them a fraction of America's minimum wage? A common answer on the left is 'exploitation.' For Thomas Friedman the answer is 'collaboration'—or 'empowering individuals in the developing world as never before.'"[7]

Globalization 3.0 isn't about *empowered individuals*, as Friedman asserts without backing up that assertion; it's about transnational corporations being totally deregulated, above the control of any nation-state, and being able to exploit poor people in developing countries and, in the process, bringing down the wages of individuals in developed countries.

When laws in the United States began making it prohibitive for corporations to exploit employees and the environment, they began moving their operations to countries which did not have these "harsh constraints." A Dickensonian capitalist's dream come true.

Friedman's *laissez-faire* free market Globalization 3.0 isn't about individuals; it's not about the people; it's *by the transnational corporation, of the transnational corporation and for the transnational corporation.*

Chapter 2:
The Ten Forces That Flattened the World

Friedman identifies ten forces that have produced this new socio-economic paradigm. Friedman could have saved his readers 233 pages of bafflegab if he had simply stated that the drivers of globalization in the twenty-first century include:

1. *Containerized Cargo Shipping* since 1956. "The Box," the standardized shipping container radically reduced the cost of shipping and removed or reduced distance as a barrier to trade;
2. *Continuing Advances in Global Communications* that began with the 1957 launch of the Sputnik satellite, and now include fiber-optic and coaxial cables, faxes, cell phones, TV and the Internet; and
3. *Cheap Labor* made available since the 1979 opening of China to capitalism, followed by India and the former Soviet Union.

Maybe a presentation and analysis of these three drivers could fill a single newspaper column, but would that sell millions of books? Where's the big money in a short, clearly written column? So let the story telling begin. Let's see? Perhaps ten "flatteners" could be conjured up. That could be just enough to spin some of the stories people love to repeat at cocktail parties.

And, so what if most of the stories and ideas are repetitions of the original stories and ideas from the dot-com era. To Friedman, what's old is new again, for in the dot-com days, the stories were about a new digital platform where you must "plug and play," "connect and collaborate," change your business model, and learn the new skills of the digital world, including right-brain "experiences"—

else you'll be toast. But no matter, Friedman identified ten flatteners, so let's look at what they are and their implications on globalization and the world.

(1) 11/9/89 (Fall of the Berlin Wall)

Wikipedia: The fall of the Berlin Wall (9th November, 1989) and the advent of PCs and Windows software have produced a global unification under the auspices of capitalism.

Here's what Matt Taibbi of the *New York Press* had to say about Friedman's first flattener, "Flattener #1 is actually two flatteners, the collapse of the Berlin Wall and the spread of the Windows operating system. In a Friedman book, the reader naturally seizes up in dread the instant a suggestive word like 'Windows' is introduced; you wince, knowing what's coming, the same way you do when Leslie Nielsen orders a Black Russian. And Friedman doesn't disappoint. His description of the early 90s:

"'The walls had fallen down and the Windows had opened, making the world much flatter than it had ever been—but the age of seamless global communication had not yet dawned.'

"How the f--- do you open a window in a fallen wall? More to the point, *why* would you open a window in a fallen wall? Or did the walls somehow fall in such a way that they left the windows floating in place to be opened? Four hundred and 73 pages [first edition] of this, folks. Is there no God?"[8]

Why does Friedman cite 1989 and the fall of the Berlin Wall as a great flattener? All it did was to flatten individuals and put more Soviets than ever into extreme poverty. "Almost a decade after [free market] reforms began, the place is a mess. Around 60 million people in Russia, almost half the population, live below the poverty line. Income inequality has risen; life expectancy has plummeted. Corruption is massive and endemic."[9]

Nobel-prize winning economist, Dr. Joseph Stiglitz, wrote in the *Guardian*, "The move from communism to capitalism in Russia after 1991 was supposed to bring unprecedented prosperity. It did not. By the time of the rouble crisis of August 1998, output had fallen by almost half and poverty had increased from 2% of the population to over 40%."[10] It seems the fall of the Berlin wall was a flattener, all right, but not the kind that Friedman wants to triumph.

Rather than 1989, 1979 was the real tipping point for opening up socialist economies to capitalism. In July 1977, Deng Xiaoping was reinstated to all the Party and government posts from which he had been dismissed during Mao Zedong's cultural revolution. The Third Plenary Session of the 11th Central Committee, held at the end of 1978, represented a great turning point of profound significance in the history of "New China." Xiaoping will be remembered for embracing capitalism by saying that "Whether a cat is black or white makes no difference. As long as it catches mice, it is a good cat." Since 1979, the Middle Kingdom has shifted its focus. Major efforts have been made to readjust the economic structure, and to reform the economic and political systems.

In fact, the "communist capitalists" have great advantages over the deregulated form of free market ideologies fostered by Wall Street and the Washington Consensus, for the Chinese government intervenes at all levels to bring about competitive advantage, including currency manipulation. Try suing to protect your intellectual property rights in China. Then, try starting an independent, democratic labor union in China. China has the People's Liberation Army and the All-China Federation of Trade Unions, where the union locals are often headed by someone from company management. Or try starting a protest over toxic working environments or unsafe equipment. According to Harold Meyerson, writing in the *Washington Post*, "The leaders of 'genuine workers' movements in China don't end up running the All-China Federation. They're to be found in prison, in exile or in hiding."[11]

At its current rate of growth, China's GDP will be twice that of America by 2050. The Chinese have a national economic strategy. Washington does not—its policies are set by the "free-market" transnational corporations exercising their powerful and untold influence.

(2) 8/9/95 (When Netscape Went Public)

Wikipedia: The confluence of the Internet, email, and web browsers, together with the "overinvestment" in optical fiber that occurred during the dot-com bubble, have produced a new template for economic activity.

Of course, none of the Netscape IPO story is news, and the real question is, did the Netscape IPO equal the breakthrough? Where was the credit really due? In the 2006 second edition of his book, Friedman had to do some backtracking caused by his earlier oversights. He renamed this section "The New Age of Connectivity: When the Web Went Around and Netscape Went Public," with more attention to Tim Berners-Lee and the creation of the Internet.

The fundamental concepts of manipulating information and managing sources of knowledge the way we do by using the World Wide Web far precedes the Internet. In a 1945 *Atlantic Monthly* article, "As We May Think," Vannevar Bush wrote, "The human mind operates by association. With one item in its grasp, it snaps instantly to the next that is suggested by the association of thoughts, in accordance with some intricate web of trails carried by the cells of the brain. It has other characteristics, of course; trails that are not frequently followed are prone to fade, items are not fully permanent, memory is transitory. Yet the speed of action, the intricacy of trails, the detail of mental pictures, is awe-inspiring beyond all else in nature."

Fast forward to the 1990s where people started putting teeth into Vannevar Bush's ideas, making his associations real via "hyperlink technology." To keep an eye on the emerging Web technology standards, Tim Berners-Lee created the World Wide Web Consortium (W3C) in 1994. While Apple Computer was the first to use hypertext with its *HyperCard* application in 1987, it was Berners-Lee who took it to the next level by networking hyperlinks on a grand scale. Thanks to Berners-Lee's World Wide Web, we now have the hyperlinked Internet.

Friedman's observation that there was an overcapacity of optical fiber networks built during the dot-com era is correct. However, this event has similarities to Britain's "Railway Mania," in the 1840s where the price of railway company shares increased, and more and more money was poured into them until the inevitable collapse. But after the bubble, a vast expansion of the British railway system ensued. It is the same for today's fiber market. As reported in Wikipedia, "Until recently, no telco would sell dark fiber (installed, but unused fiber), as selling access to this core asset was regarded as commercial suicide. However, this attitude has changed due to the enormous overcapacity installed in the ground, and dark fiber is now available for sale on the wholesale market." There is much speculation that Google is buying up dark fiber to build its own global network, bypassing the telecom players who are jockeying for continuing their monopoly-like position. The bottom line is that the world is now wired, and humankind is just now learning to harness the World Wide Web to connect computers and people in ways never before possible.

(3) Work Flow Software

Wikipedia: The extension of common Web-based standards has become operational. (From these first three "forces" results what Friedman calls "the Genesis moment for the flattening of the world.")

Friedman is clearly misinformed when he writes about workflow software to such an extent that he doesn't know its correct spelling. It's not "work flow [sic] software," it's *workflow software*.

In fact, if you search Wikipedia, the only reference to "work flow software" is Friedman's erroneous spelling.

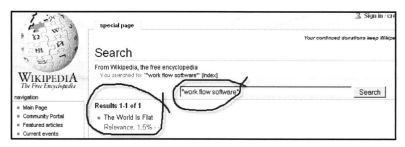

So, before rushing out to buy such software to join Friedman's supposed flat world, be sure you spell it correctly. Better yet, don't waste your time, for technology has moved far beyond workflow.

Although he had famous technology tutors, it seems Friedman didn't fully grasp what they were saying or the information they were providing him. A quick check at Wikipedia reveals that "Workflow at its simplest is the movement of documents and/or tasks through a work process. More specifically, workflow is the operational aspect of a work procedure: how tasks are structured, who performs them, what their relative order is, how they are synchronized, how information flows to support the tasks and how tasks are being tracked."

Workflow technology dates to the mid-1970s, and it didn't flatten the world. It just made big companies more powerful. An even earlier form of workflow-like technology, Electronic Data Interchange (EDI), has been around since the 1960s, with large corporations using it on their private networks to streamline the interactions between them and their trading partners. The first approaches toward workflow office-automation emerged in the 1970s.

So, the concept of workflow automation has been around for a long time. During this time, it has been often touted as a software category that will change the way people work. However, over the years, proprietary workflow automation has not managed to break-out from a concept to a widely used software category with a prominent position at the forefront of the IT landscape.

If you want your company to collaborate in the twenty-first century business environment, proprietary workflow systems of the past aren't the answer; it's business process management or BPM. BPM incorporates workflow but goes much further, making it one of today's most sought after categories of software. Friedman should have learned this from his hi-tech mentors, or at least from a visit to Wikipedia.

What Friedman would have also learned from the Wikipedia entry on BPM is that the future of twenty-first-century business collaboration deals with what is, so-far, uncharted territory, the human interaction management system. Again, from Wikipedia, "Although the initial focus of BPM was on the automation of *mechanistic* business processes, this has since been extended to integrate *human-driven* processes in which human interaction takes place in series or parallel with the mechanistic processes. A common form is where individual steps in the business process which require human intuition or judgment to be performed are assigned to the appropriate members of an organization (as with workflow systems). More advanced forms are in supporting the complex interaction between human workers in performing a workgroup task. In the latter case an emerging class of BPM software known as the Human Interaction Management System is used to support and monitor these processes as well as to permit their ongoing redefinition at runtime." [12]

Because it's people, not processes, who do work, human interaction management systems, just now emerging, will set the stage for building what IBM calls "the globally integrated enterprise," on a scale never before imaginable. So, please don't rush out and try to buy Friedman's "work flow software." It won't move you forward, but it will set you back a decade or so.

(4) Open-Sourcing

Wikipedia: *(In 2006, retitled 'Uploading')* Self-organizing collaborative communities are evolving, e.g., Apache, Wikipedia, *and blogging/podcasting* allowing people to expand and broaden knowledge free of barriers. "Of all the ten forces flattening the world, uploading has the potential to be the most disruptive."

Friedman didn't exactly get it right in the first edition, so he added new buzzwords to the second edition. You may recall, that during the dot-com era, everybody had to have a Web site. Now, Friedman implies, everyone in a flat world has to have a blog and they must start podcasting. It's interesting that most bloggers give up after a few rounds. Sure they can put their blogs out for millions to read, but *most* blogs have an interesting statistic: "Comments [0]." That's right, zero. Many people wanted to do e-commerce in the dot-com heyday, so they set up Web sites. Nobody came. They built it, but unlike the movie, *Field of Dreams,* they didn't come.

Ditto blogs and podcasts. Sure, if Thomas Friedman set up a blog, millions would likely flock to it, for he is part of Big Media, which controls the mindshare of the general public. And, as an aside, you cannot read Friedman's own column (a print blog) online unless you pay *The New York Times*. Thus Friedman, himself, isn't free to "collaborate horizontally" and upload as he sees fit; he too is controlled by his employer. It's still all about the money—the money for *The New York Times* (TimesSelect) and for Tom.

According to Friedman, if someone uploads an encyclopedia entry at Wikipedia, would they or would they not be flattened? When Friedman writes about "... *blogging/podcasting* allowing people to expand and broaden knowledge free of barriers," tell that to the blogger who was just arrested and incarcerated by the Chinese government, thanks to Yahoo. Yes, Yahoo played a role in his arrest, as CEO, Terry Semel, said, "We continue to be pissed off and are sorry about it."[13] So much for Friedman's "mother of all flatteners." In Friedman's words, "[O]f all the ten forces flattening the world, uploading has the potential to be the most disruptive." For Shi Tao, the journalist with the *Contemporary Trade News* in Hunan, a 10-year sentence in a Chinese prison, thanks, in part, to Yahoo, must certainly qualify as "disruptive."

What is uploading likely to mean in other contexts? The entities most likely to gain from uploading are corporations, not the individuals that do the uploading. For companies, blogs, podcasts and wikis are great tools for putting individuals to work for them. These new Web-based tools can certainly help companies like Microsoft. Microsoft has, for years, put customers to work for them by distributing beta releases of their products. And while it's true that individuals gain from being able helping to shape, at least in some small way, the products they purchase from Microsoft, these "uploaders" don't get compensated for their contributions. Microsoft, on the other hand, can claim that its CEO is Earth's richest person.

Consider one of the killer uploading sites, the new "social networking" site, MySpace.com. Hmmm? MySpace was swallowed up by Rupert Murdock's News Corporation for $580 million, and as we all know, Rupert "ain't stupid." What's this all about if uploading is supposed to set individuals free? In addition to the obvious advertising potential that enticed Murdock to spend hundreds of millions of dollars, companies are already finding means to set their avatars loose to exploit MySpace.com and its captive user-base. Claiming 69 million members, MySpace.com is certainly the best-known and most-visited social networking site and, for one week in June 2006, was the most visited site on the Web. As such, it is uniquely situated for commercial exploitation, as any number of bands, comedians, and other entertainers can attest. MySpace.com is bringing together the young demographic that marketers dream about, herding the cattle together to the slaughter so they can be sold stuff in a place where they're voluntary prisoners. As Rupert Murdock might say, "Let the uploading begin!"

(5) Outsourcing

Wikipedia: Outsourcing has become common (this was given a spur by the opportunity given to India by Y2K demands for programming, and far from impeding globalization's development, the dot-com bubble's implosion in fact "turbocharged" it). This "flattener" mainly focuses on India though and how outsourcing around the time of Y2K has benefited India's economy many times over.

How, exactly, did the dot-com bubble's implosion "turbocharge" outsourcing and globalization? According to Friedman, it was that after the telecoms crashed along with the dot-bomb, the fiber optic cables they put in place were now virtually free. That essentially says the growth in outsourcing was really an "accident" and wouldn't have happened unless the accident, the oversupply of world-wide fiber optic cables during the dot-com era, hadn't occurred.

Hmmm, that would be news to Jack Welch, GE's legendary CEO, who was introduced to the Internet by his former wife, Jane. Welch launched his "Destroy your business.com before some upstart in a Silicon Valley garage does!" campaign in 1999, and challenged all of GE's line-of-business executives to "Grow your business.com" by reinventing every aspect—buy, make and sell—of their business units. Welch "got it," realizing that the Internet is about business transformation, not about having a Web site, and GE accelerated its movement of R&D and manufacturing to Chindia (China and India).

GE was using the Internet to transform its global business well before the dot-com crash, and continued doing so after the crash. The book, *The Death of "e" and the Birth of the Real New Economy: Business Models, Technologies and Strategies for the 21st Century,* describes the events, "As the stunning collapse of the dot-coms and the prevailing economic winds led the lemmings among the brick-and-mortar companies to decimate technology budgets, GE increased IT spending in 2001 by 12 percent, to $3 billion.[14] Why did GE increase its IT budget in the midst of a major economic downturn? The answer was put in writing in GE's 2002 Key Growth Initiatives, "Digitization is the greatest growth opportunity our company has ever seen." The firm understands the new process-based battlefront of business. GE saved $1.6 billion from process digitization, roughly 16% of the $10 billion it expects to save annually by 2006. $100 million was freed up by digitizing inventory, accounts payable and receivable processes (operational hyper-efficiency), and a salesperson can handle up to twice as many customers (hyper-effectiveness). GE has downsized its Schenectady, New York labs established by Thomas Edison, opened a huge research facility in Shanghai and its back offices are today more likely than not located in Bangalore, India."

So it's unclear how the dot-com bubble's implosion in fact "turbocharged" outsourcing as Friedman claims. That trend was well established prior to any bubble popping. The outsourcing of white-collar work was, and still is, an established strategy used by transnational corporations to cut labor costs to the bone wherever possible.

Outsourcing is typically defined as the contracting of business operations or jobs from internal production within a business to an external entity, such as a subcontractor, that specializes in that operation. Outsourcing usually involves transferring management control to the supplier, and it requires a considerable degree of interaction and coordination. One of the major benefits of outsourcing is that the company avoids paying its employees' benefits and overhead costs, thus further reducing costs.

This is also why another of Friedman's pet words, "homesourcing" is just more bafflegab. It is because employees that work from home are still employees, e.g., at JetBlue; they are simply "telecommuting" to work. Telecommuting is a term that has been in use since the 1970s to describe working at home using a computer connected to the employer's network. Would Friedman, similarly, call a traveling salesman, "roadsourcing?"

Rather than make up new words, it should be clear that outsourcing can take many forms, but outsourcing is outsourcing, even when the external company may come to your premises to do the outsourced work. Outsourcing isn't new, so why make up words such as "insourcing?" Just to arrive at ten flatteners? On the other hand, poppycock and buzzwords make for great conversation at cocktail parties.

Does Friedman ever quit making stuff up? In a May 2006 *New York Times* column titled, "Outsourcing, Schmoutsourcing! Out Is Over," he wrote, "It's called 'around sourcing' instead of outsourcing, because there is no more 'out' anymore. Out is over." Enough already, globalization is far too serious a subject for silly neologisms.

Outsourcing is one major means of seeking the lowest possible cost of labor ("sweatshopping" is another). What's growing at an increasingly rapid rate is the outsourcing of white-collar or knowledge work. As Intel's co-founder, Andy Grove said, "Although mainstream economic thought holds that America's history of creativity and entrepreneurialism will allow it to adapt to the rise of such emerging economies as India and China, I think that is so much wishful thinking. Globalization will not only finish off what's left of American manufacturing, but will turn so-called knowledge workers, which were supposed to be America's competitive advantage, into just another global commodity."[15]

Transnational corporations, such as IBM, are going beyond outsourcing and reinventing their organizations as "globally integrated enterprises." Replacing the former model of multinational corporations having international hubs, each redundant with administrative and other overhead costs, the globally integrated enterprise is one big company that can allocate resources for local purposes or for export. IBM already has 45,000 employees in India. These consultants, developers, engineers and researchers cost a fraction of their former counterparts in America, and can be deployed in the Indian market, or called to task for projects anywhere on the planet, including Indiana. Meanwhile, back in America, *Network World* magazine reported the 2002 numbers from IBM's U.S. securities and exchange filings, "IBM layoff tally to hit 15,600."

So, call it outsourcing, insourcing, homesourcing, ruralsourcing, Schmoutsourcing, around sourcing or the globally integrated enterprise, the search by transnational corporations for the lowest-cost human supply chain is on. Damn the American middle class torpedoes, full speed ahead.

(6) Offshoring

Wikipedia: Offshoring, i.e., moving factories (China joins WTO in 2001; "China is … simply racing everyone to the bottom," China's advantages are "overwhelming") Friedman, likens the day that China officially joined the World Trade Organization as the day that the world competitively began to "run faster and faster", much like gazelles and lions run to keep their own competitive balance in nature.

The "China event," i.e., opening itself to capitalism, occurred in 1979. So what has China's 2001 membership in the WTO got to do with anything flat? China did its economic restructuring well prior to 2001 and uses the WTO to its advantage, unlike many developing countries that are being trampled by the WTO.

The really big flattener that can come under the term "offshoring" occurred long ago. April 6, 2006 was the 50th anniversary of "the box," the standardized cargo container. The box was the big one, the mother of all flatteners that launched twenty-first century globalization.

Except for products and services that are purely digital, e.g., software, information and music, the other side of the global commerce coin is physical distribution. So, let's take a deeper look at the role of physical distribution in the globalization phenomenon.

While computers and the Internet capture our imagination as the greatest technological achievements of the 20th century, a taken-for-granted marvel of our times, and cornerstone of accelerating globalization, is the jumbo jet and the cargo ship. While the Internet can bring information from anywhere in less than 2 seconds, today's air cargo jumbo jets can bring physical goods from anywhere in 36 hours, revolutionizing logistics and just-in-time supply chain management. In its all-cargo version, the new Airbus A380-800F will be the first commercial freighter with three full cargo decks—offering the unprecedented capability to carry a 150-ton payload over distances of 5,600 miles. And let's not ignore jumbo cargo ships that kick in when jet speeds don't matter, but when costs matter a lot.

On April 26, 1956, a converted tanker, the *SS Ideal-X,* left the Port of Newark, New Jersey, for the Port of Houston, Texas, carrying 58 35-foot containers, along with a regular load of liquid cargo. The Maritime Man of the Century, Malcom McLean, flew to Houston to be on hand when his ship safely docked. As the *Ideal-X* left the Port of Newark, Freddy Fields, a top official of the International Longshoremen's Association, was asked what he thought of the newly-fitted container ship. Fields replied, "I'd like to sink that son-of-a-bitch." In 1956, most cargo was loaded and unloaded by hand by longshoremen. Hand loading a ship cost $5.86 a ton at that time. Using containers, it costs only 16 cents a ton to load a ship today, a 36-fold savings.

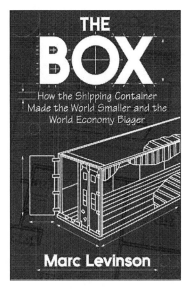

The "box," the standardized container, would ultimately mean that the China's Pearl Delta and Pittsburgh, Pennsylvania are now next-door neighbors in the same industrial park. On July 11, 2005 Samsung Heavy Industries (SHI) delivered two 9,300 TEU (twenty-foot equivalent unit) container ships to its client after holding a christening ceremony. SHI broke its own previous Guinness World Record for producing the world's largest ships, its 8,500 TEU container ships in July 2004. China's serfdom labor rates wouldn't have counted for much in the world of comparative advantage without the box.

Although Friedman's exposition on outsourcing centers on India, it is really about corporations searching the world for serfdom-level wages. There's another side to the outsourcing coin, illegal immigration, which is the great American debate of 2006. Perhaps Friedman might invent yet another neologism, *onshoring,* to describe the wage flattening impact of illegal immigration.

(7) Supply-chaining

Wikipedia: Supply-chaining ("collaborating horizontally—among suppliers, retailers, and customers—to create value,") of which Wal-Mart serves as an example.

Think about it. What does Friedman's "collaborating horizontally" actually mean as opposed to simply, "collaboration" or "collaborating?" Are there other ways to collaborate besides horizontally? Is the opposite vertical collaboration? Or non-horizontal collaboration? To fully understand Wal-Mart's mastery of "supply-chaining," see the discussion above on "offshoring," and "the box." A big-box retailer goes to China to exploit 20¢ per hour factory labor and brings the products to America in big-box containers, on big-box container ships, to sell the stuff in big-box stores across America. Full stop.

Wal-Mart was the first to exploit "Made in China," just after Sam Walton's "Made in America" marketing campaign when American manufacturing jobs were being sent to Asia in the 1980s. So, the miracle of Wal-Mart's supply chain management isn't just their advanced inventory control computer systems. It's going to the ends of the Earth, literally, to find the lowest-cost supplier. Fast forward to 2004, when Wal-Mart's Xu Jun told the *China Business Daily,* "If Wal-Mart were an individual economy, it would rank as China's eighth-biggest trading partner, ahead of Russia, Australia and Canada."

With regard to collaboration with suppliers, retailers and customers, Wal-Mart is not unique, for almost all modern companies use supply-chain–management software for collaboration. Supply-chain software has been available to large corporations for years, allowing trading partners to share demand and supply data. Supply-chain software companies have been bringing *visibility, collaboration, planning* and *control* to diverse industries: aerospace and defense, automotive, consumer industries, high-tech, industrial, metals, retail, transportation and logistics. One of the key areas pioneered by supply-chain-management software was the shift of the business model from "make to forecast" to "make to demand." These are vital topics Friedman misses in his discussion of supply-chaining.

So to restrict the discussion of supply-chaining to Wal-Mart and eating sushi in Arkansas misses the essence of the state of the art in supply-chaining.

Though Friedman seems to have just discovered the world of supply chain management, it's really quite old news. Exploring the new make-to-demand business models would have been much more supportive for his case. Supply-chaining is old hat—it's make-to-forecast, supply-push business management. Newer forms of demand-pull, make-to-demand, such as the Japanese "Kanban" real-time signaling systems, business models are the future and are the replacement for the old fashioned supply-chaining to which Friedman alerts us in his out-of-date discussion.

(8) Insourcing

Wikipedia: Insourcing, i.e. servicing supply chains, "third-party-managed logistics" (UPS).

Breaking news: Paper shredding can now be "insourced" ... or is that outsourced? ... or should we make up yet another word?

Now, what if we ship paper off-shore for shredding, then do we now have "offshore outsourcing" or is it "offshore insourcing?" Is domestic shredding unflat while offshore shredding is an integral part of the new flat world?

As we wrote in the section on outsourcing, it should be clear that outsourcing can take many forms, but outsourcing is outsourcing, even when the external company may come to your premises to do the outsourced work. While it's true that some people use the term insourcing to refer to maintaining tight control over select critical production operations, the net effect is the same as outsourcing—either your company does the work, or you hire an outside firm to do it for you. Again, whatever you wish to call it, outsourcing, insourcing, homesourcing, ruralsourcing, Schmoutsourcing, or around sourcing the goal of hiring-out work to specialists for cost savings is the same.

(9) In-forming

By in-forming Friedman means "the ability to build and deploy your own personal supply chain—a supply chain of information, knowledge, and entertainment," and Google is taken as an exemplification of these possibilities ("Google is like God," says Alan Cohen, VP of Airespace).

Sure, search engines have been instrumental in creating a fully informed customer, and as we know, information is power. We are seeing a shift from "supply-push" by producers to "demand-pull" by customers. Because consumers can now be more fully informed, thanks to Internet search capabilities, they are but one click away from going to a competitor if your company doesn't have the best offer. This shift in power—from producer to consumer—is a most important "in-forming" concept, but is one that Friedman fails to address. Instead, he talks about how a Google user informed a friend that the guy she met at a restaurant for a date had a felony assault record.

Friedman gets further carried away with the power of searching, "How does searching fit into the concept of collaboration? I call it 'in-forming.' In-forming is the individual's personal analog to open-sourcing, outsourcing, insourcing, supply-chaining, and offshoring. In-forming is the ability to build and deploy your own personal supply chain—a supply chain of information, knowledge, and entertainment. In-forming is about self-collaboration, becoming your own self-directed and self-empowered researcher, editor, and selector of entertainment, without having to go to the library or the movie theater or through network television. In-forming is searching for knowledge. It is about seeking like-minded people and communities."

Okay, let's say you want to collaborate horizontally and build your own personal supply chain with Thomas Friedman about the flat world. Go Google "Thomas Friedman" + "flat world" and start collaborating!

Any luck yet?

By the way, you might be better off forgetting Google, and use www.anywho.com where you can get his Bethesda telephone number and address, or you can write him at the Washington bureau of *The New York Times*.

Hmm, perhaps Thomas is right that in-forming "is about self-collaboration" and is the *"personal* analog to open-sourcing, outsourcing, insourcing, supply-chaining, and offshoring." What the heck is Friedman talking about, anyway? Didn't your parents warn you about self-collaboration when you were a teenager coming into puberty?

Maybe his insights on horizontal collaboration will help clear things up, "In the age of the superpower search, everyone is a celebrity. Google levels information—it has no class boundaries or education boundaries. 'If I can operate Google, I can find anything,' said Alan Cohen, vice president of Airespace, which sells wireless technology. 'Google is like God. God is wireless, God is everywhere, and God sees everything. Any questions in the world, you ask Google.'"

This sounds like the stuff of science fiction: the all-seeing god—Google—giving us salvation (information) via the wireless Internet.

(10) Amplifying technologies, or "steroids"

Wikipedia: By "steroids" Friedman means amplifying technologies like increased computing speed, file sharing, additional devices, and especially wireless.

Friedman lets us in on a secret—that technology advances—or at least, it seems that he did not think that we knew that it does. Friedman writes, "I call certain new technologies the steroids because they are amplifying and turbocharging all the other flatteners. They are taking all the forms of collaboration highlighted in this section—outsourcing, offshoring, open-sourcing, supply-chaining, insourcing, and in-forming—and making it possible to do each and every one of them in a way that is digital, mobile, virtual, and personal."

Here is one of the benefits of these turbocharged amplifiers: Now you can be put to work while you are on vacation! Unfortunately, many of us are painfully aware of this *benefit* of collaboration.

It's all about a new form of steroid. In this section, Friedman explains the *übersteroid:* wireless. Friedman concludes, "Wireless is what will allow you take everything that has been digitized, made virtual and personal, and do it from anywhere."

Now, that may be true in Korea, where the government has insured that the country is number one in broadband penetration, and is using advanced WiBro (Wireless Broadband). WiBro is a wireless broadband internet technology being developed by the Korean telecoms industry. In February 2002, the Korean government allocated 100 MHz of electromagnetic spectrum in the 2.3 GHz band, and in late 2004, WiBro Phase 1 was standardized by the Telecommunications Technology Association of Korea.

At top speed, Korea's broadband connections over very high speed digital subscriber lines (VDSL), are, on average, four times faster than the fastest U.S. broadband connections that companies like Comcast, Time Warner or the Baby Bells provide over cable modems. "Within two and a half years, we expect more than 70 percent of our households will have Internet connections with access speeds of 20 megabits per second, which will allow them to download movies to watch on their high-definition TVs," says Chin Daeje, Korea's Minister of Information and Communications and a former Samsung executive. "By 2010, the bulk of Korean households would have migrated to 100 megabits per second."

"Now Chin is aiming to leverage Korea's leadership in broadband to open up a lead in other technologies, from home networking to digital media. He doesn't have any American ideological hang-ups about the relationship between government and business. He sees his role as chief facilitator for Samsung, LG, SK Telecom and KT to help them become dominant technology players. Although movies and videos on demand are still pie in the sky in the U.S. because of slow download speeds and high costs, they are a reality in Korea. For just 80 cents, you can download a Korean hit movie in not much more than a minute. 'What Apple's iTunes is doing to music in the U.S., broadband did to movies and TV in Korea two years ago,' says Lee Jae Woong, CEO of Daum, Korea's largest Internet portal."[16]

There's even more on the horizon for Korea's broadband leadership. Korea Telecom is creating a WiBro network with the cell-to-cell roaming capabilities of regular cell phones. This means that users can not only gain wireless broadband access from traditional WiFi or WiMax hot spots, but, Samsung, the world's third-largest cell phone vendor, has demonstrated, that WiBro can also reach up to 2 Mbps inside a car moving at 120 kilometers per hour. Isn't America supposed to be the innovator and the most technologically advanced country?

Friedman forgets to mention that America ranks number 16 in broadband penetration, thanks in part to telecom deregulation that handed over decisions to the deregulated "free market."

Korea has Friedman's übersteroid, America does not.

Verizon and other telcos are changing from using copper wires to using fiber-optic cables all the way to the home. But here's the catch. In June 2006, Verizon's and the other telecoms' lobbyists were successful in getting Congress to vote against a "Network Neutrality" telecom bill amendment on a 321 to 101 vote. Net Neutrality? In short, *not* having net neutrality is like having toll booths on interstate highways, where only those who pay can use the fast express lanes, everyone else is limited to the slower local lanes.

Stanford law professor, Lawrence Lessing explains, "Net neutrality means simply that all like Internet content must be treated alike and move at the same speed over the network [the same way all vehicles on an interstate highway move at the same speed, depending of traffic conditions]. The owners of the Internet's wires cannot discriminate. This is the simple but brilliant "end-to-end" design of the Internet that has made it such a powerful force for economic and social good: All of the intelligence and control is held by producers and users, not the networks that connect them.

"The protections that guaranteed network neutrality have been law since the birth of the Internet—right up until last year, when the Federal Communications Commission eliminated the rules that kept cable and phone companies from discriminating against content providers. This triggered a wave of announcements from phone company chief executives that they plan to do exactly that.

"The implications of permanently losing network neutrality could not be more serious. The current legislation, backed by companies such as AT&T, Verizon and Comcast, would allow the firms to create different tiers of online service. They would be able to sell access to the express lane to deep-pocketed corporations and relegate everyone else to the digital equivalent of a winding dirt road. Worse still, these gatekeepers would determine who gets premium treatment and who doesn't. Their idea is to stand between the content provider and the consumer, demanding a toll to guarantee quality delivery.

"It's what Timothy Wu, an Internet policy expert at Columbia University, calls 'the Tony Soprano business model.' By extorting protection money from every Web site—from the smallest blogger to Google—network owners would earn huge profits. Meanwhile, they could slow or even block the Web sites and services of their competitors or those who refuse to pay up. They'd like Congress to 'trust them' to behave. Without net neutrality, the Internet would start to look like cable TV. A handful of massive companies would control access and distribution of content, deciding what you get to see and how much it costs."[17]

Wireless, an übersteroid in America? Maybe one day, but first, you may have to pay the phone company "protection money."

Chapter 3: The Triple Convergence

Wikipedia: Friedman argues that a triple convergence has taken place of (1) "a global, Web-enabled playing field that allows for multiple forms of collaboration … open today to more people in more places on more days in more ways than anything like it ever before in the history of the world," (2) development of new ways to collaborate horizontally, and (3) the opening up of the societies of "China, India, Russia, Eastern Europe, Latin America, and Central Asia." This "triple convergence" is "the most important force shaping global economics and politics in the early twenty-first century." Globalization will be increasingly driven by individuals. Friedman profiles "Zippies," i.e., Indians who have come of age since India embraced capitalism. His discussion of China focuses on student visas, of Russia on the experience of Boeing. These developments were obscured, however, by "the other triple convergence," viz. the dot-com bust, 9/11, and the Enron-related business scandals.

After telling readers how he discovered you could print your Southwest Airlines boarding pass at home, which he interprets as Southwest *collaborating* with its customers and they with Southwest in a new way, and telling about his favorite commercial for the Minolta Konica machine that allows you to do black-and-white or color printing, copy a document, fax it, scan it, scan it to e-mail, or Internet-fax it—all from the same machine, Friedman finally reveals Convergence I of his Triple Convergence. "This is what I mean when I say the world has been flattened. It is the complementary convergence of the ten flatteners, creating this new global playing field for multiple forms of collaboration."

Friedman must have been sleeping to have just now discovered the ingredients he claims make for Convergence I. It's fairly common knowledge that Southwest and other airlines let their customers print boarding passes at home, and all-in-one print, fax, scan, and copy machines have been readily available to both businesses and consumers for years. Convergence II? Well Friedman never really defines it, but he does write about big spurts, "Introducing new technology alone is never enough. The big spurts in productivity come when a new technology is combined with new ways of doing business." This must mean that when companies figure out what to do with the new technology, then Convergence II has occurred?

Let's move on to Convergence III. "Just as we finished creating this new, more horizontal playing field, and companies and individuals primarily in the West started quickly adapting to it, 3 billion people who had been frozen out of the field suddenly found themselves liberated to plug and play with everybody else."

Wow, wouldn't you like to have the contract for all those machines and networks that would be needed to outfit those 3 billion new workers that Friedman proclaims are now ready to "plug and play" and to "connect and collaborate?" Are these 3 billion people really liberated to plug and play with everybody else? The reality is that 99.5% of these 3 billion new flat worlders simply don't have access to the Internet and to Friedman's plug and play playground. He does get a little more specific with his numbers, as he first cuts the 3 billion in half to 1.5 billion and then divides that by ten. "True, maybe only 10 percent of this new 1.5 billion-strong workforce (oops, where did the other 1.5 billion people go?) entering the global economy have the education and connectivity to collaborate and compete at a meaningful level. But that is still 150 million people, roughly the size of the entire U.S. workforce." This means that 1.35 billion sweatshop workers doing duty 10 hours a day, 7 days a week for 20¢ an hour have been added to the transnational corporations' workforce—now they can *sweat and play* in Friedman's new neoliberal utopia. And, doing the math in his flat-world analysis, 1.5 billion people outside his 1.5 billion-strong workforce have just vanished into thin air—or you could say they just got flattened. That's surely one way to optimize the "new global playing field for multiple forms of collaboration" he calls Convergence I.

But also keep in mind that, according to Friedman, Convergence III diminishes the role of global economic institutions. "We tend to think of global trade and economics as something driven by the IMF, the G-8, the World Bank, the WTO, and the trade treaties forged by trade ministers. I don't want to suggest that these governmental agencies are irrelevant. They are not. But they are going to become less important. In the future globalization is going to be increasingly driven by the individuals who understand the flat world, adapt themselves quickly to its processes and technologies, and start to march forward—without any treaties or advice from the IMF. They will be every color of the rainbow and from every corner of the world."

"The global economy from here forward will be shaped less by the ponderous deliberations of finance ministers and more by the spontaneous explosion of energy from the zippies. Yes, Americans grew up with the hippies in the 1960s. Thanks to the high-tech revolution, many of us became yuppies in the 1980s. Well, now let me introduce the zippies."

"'The Zippies Are Here,' declared the Indian weekly magazine *Outlook*. Zippies are the huge cohort of Indian youth who are the first to come of age since India shifted away from socialism and dived headfirst into global trade and the information revolution by turning itself into the world's service center. *Outlook* called India's zippies 'Liberalization's Children' and defined a zippie as a 'young city or suburban resident, between 15 and 25 years of age, with a zip in the stride. Belongs to Generation Z. Can be male or female, studying or working. Oozes attitude, ambition and aspiration. Cool, confident and creative. Seeks challenges, loves risks and shuns fear.' Indian zippies feel no guilt about making money or spending it. They are, says one Indian analyst quoted by *Outlook*, 'destination driven, not destiny driven, outward looking, not inward, upwardly mobile, not stuck-in-my-station-in-life.' With 54 percent of India under the age of twenty-five—that's 555 million people—six out of ten Indian households have at least one potential zippie. And the zippies don't just have a pent-up demand for good jobs; they want the good life."

The Triple Convergence is now complete. Ladies and gentlemen, welcome to the Friedman's Flat World. As a mere mortal, you should take this quite seriously, for remember what professor Roberto J. Gonzalez had to say, "Over the past 15 years, Thomas Friedman's writing has influenced presidents, policy-makers and captains of industry across the world." You had better not be a doubting Thomas. Move over IMF, G-8, World Bank, and WTO; the Zippies are coming.

Chapter 4: The Great Sorting Out

Wikipedia: Friedman pays tribute to Marx as analyst of capitalism, at the suggestion of Prof. Michael Sandel of Harvard University. He discusses, rather uncritically, the nature of corporations, and argues that in the new paradigm that is developing hierarchies will be undermined. But social responsibilities do not always jibe with political attitudes. New property issues to resolve have arisen). Communication is reduced to more impersonal means. And important values questions remain.

Friedman, a Marxist? This may get interesting. True, the first 233 pages of the 2nd edition of Friedman's book were so convoluted that a great sorting out would be in order.

Friedman starts his great sorting out with, "Because when the world starts to move from a primarily vertical (command and control) value-creation model to an increasingly horizontal (connect and collaborate) creation model, it doesn't affect just how business gets done. It affects everything."

That unfounded assertion assumes that the zippies connect and collaborate, wresting control from previously vertical organizations. The fact that transnational corporations still "command and control" the zippies is simply ignored.

What we may be actually experiencing is the unleashing of the transnational corporation to pursue unfettered raw capitalism. This is much the way capitalism was pursued at the beginning of the Industrial Revolution, before being dampened by labor and environmental regulations.

Recognizing the capitalists' excesses during the Industrial Revolution, leaders, such as President Theodore Roosevelt, reigned in raw capitalism and created a "mixed economy," not a pure laissez-faire form of capitalism. But free-market Friedman seems to now assert that, with his utopian, digitally connected flat world, even the nation-state could wane as flat-world capitalists create, in the words of Marx and Engels, "a world after its own image." Friedman writes of his meeting with Harvard University political theorist Michael Sandel, "Sandel startled me slightly by remarking that the sort of flattening process that I was describing was actually first identified by Karl Marx and Friedrich Engels in the *Communist Manifesto*, published in 1848. Referring to the *Communist Manifesto*, Sandel told me, 'You are arguing something similar. What you are arguing is that developments in information technology are enabling companies to squeeze out all the inefficiencies and friction from their markets and business operations. That is what your notion of 'flattening' really means. But a flat, frictionless world is a mixed blessing. It may, as you suggest, be good for global business. Or it may, as Marx believed, augur well for a proletarian revolution. But it may also pose a threat to the distinctive places and communities that give us our bearings, that locate us in the world. From the first stirrings of capitalism, people have imagined the possibility of the world as a perfect market—unimpeded by protectionist pressures, disparate legal systems, cultural and linguistic differences, or ideological disagreement. But this vision has always bumped up against the world as it actually is—full of sources of friction and inefficiency. Some obstacles to a frictionless global market are truly sources of waste and lost opportunities. But some of these inefficiencies are institutions, habits, cultures, and traditions that people cherish precisely because they reflect nonmarket values like social cohesion, religious faith, and national pride. If global markets and new communications technologies flatten those differences, we may lose something important. That is why the debate about capitalism has been, from the very beginning, about which frictions, barriers, and boundaries are mere sources of waste and inefficiency, and which are sources of identity and belonging that we should try to protect. From the telegraph to the Internet, every new communications technology has promised to shrink the distance between people, to increase access to information, and to bring us ever closer to the dream of a perfectly efficient, frictionless global market. And each time, the question for society arises with renewed urgency: To what extent should we stand aside, 'get with the program,' and do all we can to squeeze out yet more inefficiencies, and to what extent should we lean against the current for the sake of values that global markets can't supply? Some sources of friction are worth protecting, even in the face of a global economy that threatens to flatten them. As Sandel argued, what I call collaboration could be seen by others as just a nice name for the ability to hire cheap labor in India."

After recognizing Sandel's arguments, Friedman goes on to build an argument that implies a diminishing role for the nation-state, "The biggest source of friction, of course, has always been the nation-state, with its clearly defined boundaries and laws. Are national boundaries a source of friction we should want to preserve, or even can preserve, in a flat world? What about legal barriers to the free flow of information, intellectual property, and capital—such as copyrights, worker protections, and minimum wages? In the wake of the triple convergence, the more the flattening forces reduce friction and barriers, the sharper the challenge they will pose to the nation-state and to the particular cultures, values, national identities, democratic traditions, and bonds of restraint that have historically provided some protection and cushioning for workers and communities. Which do we keep and which do we let melt away into air so we can all collaborate more easily? Looking at it from the American corner of the flat world, you might conclude that the frictions, barriers, and values that restrain outsourcing should be maintained, maybe even strengthened. But from the point of view of Indians, fairness, justice, and their own aspirations demand that those same barriers and sources of friction be removed. In the flat world, one person's economic liberation could be another's unemployment. India versus Indiana: Who Is Exploiting Whom?"

Friedman simply sweeps the nation-state issue under the rug by "having the political scientists sort this stuff out later." He avoids the more important issues of shifting to new geoeconomic realignments of globalizing markets that will also lead to new geopolitical realignments. Friedman oversimplifies and boils the issues down to capitalist zippies versus nation-states. This is nonsense. The issues are much broader than having one homogenized, world-wide capitalist market vs. nation-states getting in the way by creating friction.

Jagdish Sheth and Rajendra Sisodia, take these broader issues head on in *Tectonic Shift: The Geoeconomic Realignment of Globalizing Markets*. "As long as the mature, advanced economics of the U.S., Western Europe, and Japan primarily trade with each other, they will not continue to thrive. They can, however, avoid this fate if they begin integrating their economies with specific developing economies. They note that most developed countries have high prosperity but low growth, while many developing nations have high growth but low prosperity. Thus, the surest and fastest way to benefit the largest number of people is to create true synergy by speeding integration between countries from both categories.

"Market forces are already driving the growth of regional blocs, whose members are attempting to serve their mutual interests and deliver competitive advantages unavailable to nonmembers. Ultimately, three major north-south regional blocs will emerge: a US/American bloc, a European/African bloc, and an Asian bloc. These strategic partnerships will involve free trade, monetary union, cross-border infrastructure investments, regional development agencies, and conflict resolution mechanisms. The emergence of this tripolar system promises a more stable world economy than is possible when there is only one superpower, or when two superpowers are locked in irreconcilable conflict with each other."

And, don't count out the individual nation-state in the game of globalization. Some nation-states have powerful strategies, even though America does not—except for its blind ideology of starving government (don't look too closely at our national debt) and leaving economic decisions to global corporations and their lobbyists.

The bottom line is that the issues of sorting out twenty-first century style globalization, Friedman does point out some very important things about which we need to think, "Companies have never had more freedom, and less friction, in the way of assigning research, low-end manufacturing, and high-end manufacturing anywhere in the world. What this will mean for the long-term relationship between companies and the country in which they are headquartered is simply unclear. More and more, politics in the flat world will consist of asking which values, frictions, and fats are worth preserving— which should, in Marx's language, be kept solid—and which must be left to melt away into the air. Countries, companies, and individuals will be able to give intelligent answers to these questions only if they understand the real nature and texture of the global playing field and how different it is from the one that existed in the Cold War era and before."

While these are good points, today's harried citizens learn what they know from what Big Media companies decide to report, or not report. These companies and their lobbyists are in control of what gets "sorted out." For example, where was the public debate on Net Neutrality in June 2006? As Dr. Lawrence Lessing of Stanford Law School reported, "The phone companies pulled out all the stops to legislate themselves monopoly power. They spent tens of millions of dollars on inside-the-Beltway print, radio and TV ads; high-priced lobbyists; coin-operated think tanks; and sham 'Astroturf' groups— fake grass-roots operations with such Orwellian names as *Hands Off the Internet* and *NetCompetition.org*." We repeat that the vote in Congress was 321 to 101.

The Internet, Friedman's cornerstone flattener just got flattened by powerful corporations and their lobbyists. The results will mean even more control over the information available to individuals, individuals who are supposed to be the democratic foundation of power in America. Horizontal collaboration "capability" is one thing, mindshare control over the population by Big Media is quite another.

In discussing all this sorting out amongst nation-states, companies and individuals, Friedman makes no mention of global organizations such as the World Trade Organization, the IMF and the World Bank. Have they no role in the great sorting out? Of course they do, and the picture there is also unclear as to who is supposed to benefit from these organizations or exactly how they operate since most of their decisions are made behind closed doors. But what they do affects each and every one of us. As Friedman says, "Countries, companies, and individuals will be able to give intelligent answers to these questions only if they understand the real nature and texture of the global playing field and how different it is from the one that existed in the Cold War era and before." But he simply ignores these organizations in his great sorting out, even though they are perhaps the central entities sorting things out. Nor does he mention deregulated Big Media that consolidates a supposed free press into the hands of six or seven transnational corporations.

To educate yourself you'll have to move beyond Friedman and on to Joseph Stiglitz, Nobel prize winning economist and former chief economist with the World Bank, whom Friedman totally ignores. You'll also want to learn from Dr. Vandana, of the Foundation for Science, Technology & Ecology, New Delhi, India. If you want to understand the real nature and texture of the global playing field you won't find comprehensive or balanced information in Friedman's book. You'll have to read some of the following: Stiglitz, *Globalization and Its Discontents* and *Fair Trade for All;* Cavanagh and Mander, *Alternatives to Economic Globalization: A Better World Is Possible;* Prestowitz, *Three Billion New Capitalists,* and Sheth and Sisodia, *Tectonic Shift: The Geoeconomic Realignment of Globalizing Markets.*

Sorry, but the critical issues of globalization were just not properly covered by the information Friedman gathered from the friends he visits, the CEO's he knows, and the golf courses at which he plays. Friedman leaves us on our own to sort out the critical issues of globalization.

Part 2: America and the Flat World

Chapter 5: America and Free Trade

Wikipedia: The self-identified "free-trader" mentions David Ricardo's theory of comparative advantage as the theoretical underpinning justifying globalization as an economic project. Friedman acknowledges that there is currently an intense debate over the status of this theory, but opines that "Ricardo is still right." His chief reason for dismissing objections is that economics is not a zero-sum game. He admits, however, that those who are low-skilled are very vulnerable to current trends, but he expresses an abiding faith in the existence of an infinite array of human wants and needs that can endlessly fuel economic expansion. He quotes Raghuram Rajan, director of research for the International Monetary Fund, who says that "everyone wins" in a world with a "bigger but more complex pie."

Before opening the next section of his book, "America and the Flat World," Friedman closes "The Great Sorting Out" with, "Brace yourself: You are now about to enter the flat world." Thanks for the appropriate warning. We are now braced for what he is conjuring up next: "My mind just kept telling me, 'Ricardo is right, Ricardo is right, Ricardo is right.' David Ricardo (1772–1823) was the English economist who developed the free-trade theory of comparative advantage, which stipulates that if each nation specializes in the production of goods in which it has a comparative cost advantage and then trades with other nations for the goods in which they specialize, there will be an overall gain in trade, and overall income levels should rise in each trading country." Seldom has there appeared such a superficial treatment of Ricardo's "comparative advantage," that is, except perhaps in some 11th grade civics class.

Okay. Ricardo is right. "According to Ricardo's theory, even if a country could produce everything more efficiently than another country, it would reap gains from specializing in what it was best at producing and trading with other nations," writes Friedman.

And in many ways, Ricardo is also *irrelevant* to Friedman's brief history of the twenty-first century. Consider Schumer and Roberts' Op-Ed piece, in the January 6, 2004 *New York Times*, "When Ricardo said that free trade would produce shared gains for all nations, he assumed that the resources used to produce goods—what he called the 'factors of production'—would not be easily moved over international borders.

"Comparative advantage is undermined if the factors of production can relocate to wherever they are most productive: in today's case, to a relatively few countries with abundant cheap labor. In this situation, there are no longer shared gains—some countries win and others lose."

"And one thing is certain: real and effective solutions will emerge only when economists and policymakers end the confusion between the free flow of goods and the free flow of factors of production."

The notion of "pure competition," a notion often implied in free-trader Friedman's book, never has been a reality. Actually, there is very little "free" in today's free trade, and equally little "fair" with free trade.

Clyde Prestowitz, former counselor to the Secretary of Commerce in the Reagan Administration, and author of *Three Billion New Capitalists,* explains, "The real problem is that globalization is a different game for many countries than it is for America. China, along with many countries offer tax holidays, financial incentives, and protected markets to attract new facilities in 'strategic' industries. The chronically overvalued dollar and the foreign investment incentives also cause a steady transfer of production and technology abroad while putting downward pressure on wages and building large foreign claims on future U.S. income.

"David Ricardo developed his thinking on comparative advantage in the eighteenth century when things like economies of scale were pretty much unknown and were not included in much of the analysis. Even more significantly, it was assumed that technology and capital and labor don't move easily from one country to the next, that they are more or less immobile; that products move, but that capital and labor and technology are kind of indigenous. But with the Internet, anywhere in the world is just two seconds away. And, even if you work in physical stuff, FedEx can deliver anywhere in the world in, maximum, thirty-six hours. In short, time and distance have been negated. U.S. policymakers and economists have not absorbed this into their thinking. They are still operating on the basis of David Ricardo's assumptions, which essentially no longer hold together."

Prestowitz elaborates on why the world isn't flat, "It is tilted because, in this whole system, there is one consumer. The United States. We are the world's all-time champion superpower, hyperpower consumer. We consume $700 billion more than we produce. We are such great consumers that, when we go to war, our president tells us, 'Go buy more.' It is not, 'Buy war bonds,' not, 'Save,' but, 'Buy more, and by the way, here's a tax cut to help you buy more.' We really consume.

"The rest of the world are sellers—the Japanese, the Chinese, the EU. The rest of the world saves, invests, produces, exports to us, and they lend us money—kind of vendor financing—so that we can continue to buy their goods. If everybody in this game could or would guarantee to keep doing exactly what they are doing, this would be perfect. We would get to have a party indefinitely in the United States, live way above our means forever. What could be better than that? The rest of the world likes this, too, because it facilitates their development, their growth. It tends to sweep technology and sweep know-how away from the West, away from the U.S., into Asia and helps them catch up. It serves their strategic purposes."

So, comparative advantage isn't some absolute Ricardian principle. It's what you make of it. As Prestowitz points out, "the way that we are approaching globalization right now is a way in which there are really two games being played. All these countries [the Japanese, the Chinese, the EU] are members of the World Trade Organization. Many of them are members of the OECD [Organization for Economic Co-operation and Development] and the International Monetary Fund. So the presumption, and the way this is presented to the press and to the public, is that we are all playing the same game.

"But the truth is that, in the world of economics, it is a bipolar world. Part of the world is playing what I would call 'dirty free trade.' That would include us, the Canadians, the Mexicans, the EU, the Chileans, the Aussies. When I say 'dirty free trade,' what I mean is that they are not pure. We protect the sugar industry. We put tariffs on steel every once in a while. We are far from pure in our approach to free trade. But on balance, we believe in markets. The objective of our policies is essentially consumer welfare. The system is pretty transparent. We have a rule of law. We believe in competition. So it is consumer-oriented dirty free trade.

"There is a whole different set of countries, particularly in Asia, who are playing mercantilism [merchants primarily selling their stuff to America while lacking a consumption-oriented society of their own]. It is interesting to see how that works out. Does anybody want to be part of America's strategy? The answer is no. Why not? Because we don't have a strategy. That is the point.

"A number of countries have strategic economics. They do have a strategy. China happens to be one of them. It is not the only one. Singapore, Malaysia, Japan—they all have strategies. These countries that have strategies operate in the following way: They all have very high savings rates. These savings rates are high not because of Confucian principles, but because there is compulsion; there are strong incentives to save. In Singapore, they just take 40 percent of your check and put it in the Provident Fund before you get your check, and that is your savings. They all have relatively low consumption rates. It doesn't mean they are not good consumers. If you see them, as individuals, shopping, they shop like crazy. You know that, if you see a bunch of Japanese shoppers. But if you look at their GDP, consumption is not a high percentage of GDP, because, again, there are all kinds of incentives in the system to make it hard to spend that much money. So consumption is low; savings is high.

"They all have export-led growth strategies. They all are focusing explicitly on achieving growth by promoting exports. To do that, they manage the dollar. They either peg their currency or they intervene massively in exchange markets to keep the dollar artificially high against their currencies, in order to facilitate these exports.

"The objective here is to accumulate surpluses and to accumulate big dollar reserves, for the purposes that I explained earlier. This is the strategy.

"So you have one set of countries that is playing strategic economics and another set of countries that is kind of playing dirty free trade."

What does any of this have to do with Ricardo? Nothing, except that countries that get it are defining their own comparative advantage, now that time and distance don't matter. It will probably take what Prestowitz calls an "economic 9/11" for Americans to finally get it, and that will be very painful.

As Robert B. Reich, a professor at the Goldman School of Public Policy at the University of California, Berkeley, and a former United States secretary of labor points out in his review of *Fair Trade for All,* "While Stiglitz and Charlton nobly assert that trade agreements should be viewed as presumptively unfair if they bestow disproportionate benefits on richer nations, they fail to acknowledge that within richer nations free trade is already disproportionately benefiting the best educated and best connected. The wealthy are growing much wealthier while the middle class is being squeezed. In fact, the adjustment mechanisms the authors find lacking in most developing economies—good public schools, modern infrastructure and adequate social safety nets—are coming to be less and less available even in America. But until those gains are more widely shared—within richer countries as well as between richer and poorer—we can kiss any further round of trade liberalization goodbye."

Following Friedman's closing advice of "upgrading your skills and making the investment in those practices that will enable you and your society to claim your slice of the bigger but more complex pie," is, itself, pie in the sky. Many economists and sociologists argue that free trade, as practiced today, is just a euphemism for corporate imperialism and the rich getting richer—but that *fair* and free trade is a true hope for a better world, not just a hollowing out of the middle classes around the world.

Chapter 6: The Untouchables

Wikipedia: An untouchable, in Friedman's parlance, is a person whose job cannot be outsourced. According to Friedman, Untouchables come in four broad categories: workers who are "special," workers who are "specialized," workers who are "anchored," and workers who are "really adaptable." Adaptability through education is key to economic security. Friedman reviews the advantages that the United States possesses: U.S. research universities & labs, capital markets, intellectual property laws, flexible labor laws, large domestic market, political stability, and a tradition as a meeting place for cultures. (2006: Friedman adds a 16-page section, [The New Middle, discussing The New Middlers, illustrating such occupations: Great Collaborators and Orchestrators, The Great Synthesizers, The Great Explainers, The Great Leveragers, The Great Adapters, The Passionate Personalizers, and The Great Localizers]).

What, according to Friedman, should your children want to be when they grow up? Great Collaborators and Orchestrators, Great Synthesizers, Great Explainers, Great Leveragers, Great Adapters, Passionate Personalizers, or Great Localizers? Or tuba players with an engineering degree, as introduced in a whole new chapter in the second edition of Friedman's book?

Look at that list again. What Friedman seems to be telling us is that we all should become masters of social, organizational, and motivational skills. He might as well have just said, "Honey, I confessed [in a whisper], we all should become, you know, *managers!* Major in management! Send your kid to management school, with a minor in tuba playing, and all will be well."

Managers don't do work; they collaborate, orchestrate, synthesize, explain, leverage, adapt, personalize and localize. Let the Chinese and Indians do the work. We'll just manage, using our right brain, and perhaps top managers will also play the tuba. Hmm, I'm kind of liking this new flat world already.

But now, let's absorb some of the deeper wisdom of Chapter 6, "The Untouchables." "So if the flattening of the world is largely (but not entirely) unstoppable, and holds out the potential to be as beneficial to American society as a whole as past market evolutions have been, how does an individual get the best out of it? What do we tell our kids?" Now, get ready for the answer, and be prepared for a real shock, "There is only one message: You have to constantly upgrade your skills." Didn't we used to call this life-long learning?

And what exactly do you tell your kids? Tell them what Friedman told his daughters, "Girls, when I was growing up, my parents used to say to me, 'Tom, finish your dinner—people in China and India are starving.' My advice to you is: Girls, finish your homework—

people in China and India are starving for your jobs."

When Friedman retires, he can work part-time writing ads for community colleges: "Y'all come on down and upgrade your skills! And while you're at it, do some innovation, for America has some of the best intellectual property laws in the world. Come on down and do some horizontal collaboration, y'all." Lifelong learning—now there's a new concept. This whole chapter is pure clichéd nonsense.

Chapter 7: The Right Stuff (Added in the 2006 edition)

Wikipedia: Friedman identifies themes that are important for educators to emphasize in a flat world: learning how to learn, passion and curiosity, liking other people, nourishing the right brain. Georgia Tech successfully reformed itself along these lines in the 1990s. U.S. has the potential to adapt to the flat world, but so far is not doing so.

In this chapter, Friedman introduces his formula for success in his flat world: $CQ + PQ > IQ$, or one's Curiosity Quotient plus Passion Quotient is of greater importance than one's Intelligence Quotient. According to Friedman, "the first, and most important, ability is the ability to learn how to learn—to constantly absorb and teach yourself new ways of doing old things or new ways of doing new things." Thus teachers and parents should be instilling curiosity and passion in their children. And, of course, you do this by giving them access to the Web, as just about everything you want to know is out on the net. He goes on to say that, to be successful in the flat world, you need to like people and "play well with others." But, alas, he laments, "I am not sure how you teach that as part of a classroom curriculum, but someone had better figure it out."

He concludes the chapter by noting that America has all the right stuff and can succeed if "we roll up out shirtsleeves, educate our young people the right way for these times, and tend to and enrich our sauce. So, are we doing that?" His answer is, "No!" which then leads the reader to the chapters that follow.

There is so little to critique about this chapter for it, like the previous one, says so little, and what it does say is mostly clichés and simplistic solutions to quite complex and even intractable problems.

Chapter 8: The Quiet Crisis

Wikipedia: However, Friedman argues that the United States also has so many significant weaknesses that "we are in a crisis now." The U.S. is neglecting science and engineering. American youth show signs of a lack of ambition and work ethic. And foreigners are increasingly better educated.

Friedman's view of contemporary America is, in a nutshell, that "American society started to coast in the 1990s, when our third postwar generation came of age. The dot-com boom left too many people with the impression that they could get rich without investing in hard work. All it took was an MBA and a quick IPO, or one NBA contract, and you were set for life. But while we were admiring the flat world we had created, a lot of people in India, China, and Eastern Europe were busy figuring out how to take advantage of it. Lucky for us, we were the only economy standing after World War II, and we had no serious competition for forty years. That gave us a huge head of steam but also a huge sense of entitlement and complacency—not to mention a certain tendency in recent years to extol consumption over hard work, investment, and long-term thinking. When we got hit with 9/11, it was a once-in-a-generation opportunity to summon the nation to sacrifice, to address some of its pressing fiscal, energy, science, and education shortfalls—all the things that we had let slide. But our president did not summon us to sacrifice. He summoned us to go shopping. In the previous chapters, I showed why both classic economic theory and the inherent strengths of the American economy have convinced me that American individuals have nothing to worry about from a flat world—provided we roll up our sleeves, be ready to compete, get every individual to think about how he or she upgrades his or her educational skills, and keep investing in the secrets of the American sauce."

Friedman asserts that America has a numbers gap (i.e., declining numbers of scientists and engineers), an ambition gap, and an education gap. The bottom line is that 30% of American children drop out of high school, and America is falling far behind other countries in science and math education. And oh yes, the federal government is cutting monies for basic research and other traditional science investments. All of these trends have been widely reported on television news and in newspapers.

Friedman's conclusion, "… we should be embarking on an all-hands-on-deck, no-holds-barred, no-budget-too-large crash program for science and engineering education immediately. The fact that we are not doing so is our quiet crisis. Scientists and engineers don't grow on trees. They have to be educated through a long process, because, ladies and gentlemen, this really is rocket science." If you didn't already know this, you probably don't care anyway.

If we gear up, as Friedman suggests, and start turning out engineering graduates, what can they expect when they graduate? IBM just laid off 15,000 American employees and hired 45,000 Indians. Young American engineering graduates might do better if they pack their bags and move to Bangalore, because that's where their jobs are going. But they had better get used to the Bangalore pay scale, because that's why the jobs are going there.

In his "reluctant" critique of Friedman's flat-world book, Norm Matloff, a professor of computer science at the University of California at Davis writes, "I used the word 'reluctant' … not because I am reluctant [to] criticize *New York Times* journalist Thomas Friedman, but because I am reluctant to give him any publicity. I don't mind people who disagree with me, of course, but I get irritated if their views are based on snap judgments rather than careful, thorough examination of the facts. I get even more irritated if they hide the fact that they stand to gain financially from those views which they present as being for the public good. All of that is why I really don't want to give Friedman any publicity (even if my 'contribution' is tiny compared to what he already has). Friedman has always gotten lots of publicity, especially with his latest big theme, which is basically, 'Globalization is good, and its downsides can be compensated by improving our educational system.' He is one of those who, for example, hold the Alice in Wonderland view that we can solve our current problem of unemployed engineers and scientists by producing MORE engineers and scientists."[18]

He continues his thoughts in the technical journal, *Communications of the ACM*, "Even the ITAA, [Information Technology Professionals Association of America] as a staunch advocate of globalization, paints a gloomy picture for U.S. IT workers projecting that the only major sector of the U.S. economy likely to shrink over the next decade as a result of offshoring will be IT. Not to worry, says the ITAA, because the number of jobs will increase in non-IT categories (such as construction and finance). But the vast majority of these jobs will not be of the high-level variety (such as architects and financial market analysts that have begun to migrate offshore, too). Thus the U.S. would lose IT and other jobs requiring a more rigorous level of education in exchange for gaining jobs (such as carpenters and loan officers) requiring a less-demanding education. You don't have to be a rocket economist to see that such a trend would be disastrous for the U.S."

Perhaps the real issue is that America does not have a national industrial policy that identifies and strengthens the industries in which it wants to be the master in the twenty-first century. America's economic policies are, by and large, set by transnational corporations who wield excessive power in Washington. Their interests are not in America, but are in their stockholders. As more than one high-tech CEO has said, their interests may indeed lie outside of the United Sates, as clearly pointed out by Clyde Prestowitz in *Three Billion New Capitalists*. So, keeping this in mind, Friedman's thesis would translate into "Go East, young man. Get your engineering degree, and move to Bangalore, because that's where your job is going."

Chapter 9: This Is Not a Test

Wikipedia: Friedman issues a call to Americans to respond to the challenge. There is yet an unmet need for political leadership. On social issues, Friedman briefly argues that benefits and education should be "as flexible as possible;" he calls for "portable health insurance" and proclaims that he wants to see "every American man or woman on a campus." Pro-globalization advocates must recognize the need for compassionate measures, if only out of self-interest. There remains a need to sort out "the relationship between global corporations and their own moral consciences." Friedman argues there is a little-acknowledged and hard-to-see "progressive tilt" observable in the behavior of big business. Another crying need, he adds, is for "improved parenting."

"What this era has in common with the Cold War era, though, is that to meet the challenges of flatism requires as comprehensive, energetic, and focused a response as did meeting the challenge of communism. It requires our own version of the New Frontier and Great Society adapted to the age of flatness. It requires a president who can summon the nation to get smarter and study harder in science, math, and engineering in order to reach the new frontiers of knowledge that the flat world is rapidly opening up and pushing out.

And it requires a Great Society that commits our government to building the infrastructure, safety nets, and institutions that will help every American become more employable in an age when no one can be guaranteed lifetime employment. I call my own version of this approach compassionate flatism." "Compassionate flatism" has a faintly familiar ring—compassionate conservatism anyone?

In this chapter Friedman gets prescriptive. What America needs is leadership, muscles (portable benefits and opportunities for life-long learning), good fat (wage insurance), social activism, and for good measure, good parenting. Here is Friedman's advice on the last of this list, "There comes a time when you've got to put away the Game Boys, turn off the television set, put away the iPod, and get your kids down to work." Now you can certainly see why Friedman's writing has influenced presidents, policy-makers and captains of industry. We go from Friedman the economist, to Friedman the technologist, and now to Friedman the counselor of parents—that is if you are into clichés in each arena. Sure, we need leadership, economic safety nets, and good parenting, but do we require 600 pages to learn that?

But what will it take to get people in a debt-ridden, media-driven consumption society to switch off *The Simpsons* and do the hard work America needs to do to get back to the values that made us a mighty economic player? Friedman's book certainly won't do that because those consumers don't read 600-page books, and they feel entitled to be consumption kings simply because they are Americans. It's going to take the pain of what Prestowitz deems an "economic 9/11" to do that. The 1929 Great Depression 2.0 will likely trigger the real values turnaround, not just putting way our children's iPods.

Part 3: Developing Countries and the Flat World

Chapter 10: The Virgin of Guadalupe

Wikipedia: In this chapter, Friedman briefly addresses the problems of developing countries. He jokingly proposes the establishment of a "Developing Countries Anonymous (D.C.A.)" organization modeled on Alcoholics Anonymous. Top-down reform has limits in these societies, he argues. There is a need for what he calls "reform retail": "upgrading" infrastructure, regulatory institutions, education, and culture to "remove as many friction points as possible" that impede globalization. He exhorts societies to be open cultures and reject tribalism, and has special criticisms for Muslim societies. Additional, intangible factors, are social will and dynamic leadership.

Beginning with this chapter, Friedman goes from prescribing what Americans need to do about flatism to what developing countries need to do. Much of it is, as you might expect, about drinking his corporate globalism Kool-Aid. In this chapter, "The Virgin of Guadalupe," when it comes to criticizing Muslim societies and creating meaningless neologisms, e.g., Developing Countries Anonymous (DCA), Friedman is certainly no virgin. He's been there and has done that many times before.

When turning his attention to one of his favorite subjects, the Middle East, and the Arab streets, Friedman asserts, "The only new businesses are gas stations, whose owners, rarely reinvest their funds in the neighborhood. Many people on the Arab street have their curtains closed, their shutters drawn, and signs on their front lawn that say, 'No Trespassing. Beware of Dog.'" That is an odd assertion as the very last pet one is likely to find in an Arab home, in Saudi Arabia for example, is a dog. Friedman's sign would be the equivalent of "No Trespassing. Beware of Rat" on an American front lawn. Maybe both Saudi Arabia and America could really use a sign that says, "No Trespassing. Beware of Friedman!" Let's go to the Arabian peninsula and see if we can spot any of those no trespassing signs.

Hmmm, in this picture, they must have cropped out the "Beware of Dog" signs that Friedman talks about. Is this Friedman's "dark alley" that Intel's Craig Barrett is walking down in 2002? And why would Barrett be in Dubai?

Dubai has its sights set on knowledge work. Dubai Internet City provides a knowledge economy ecosystem that is designed to support the business development of Information and Communications Technology (ICT) companies. It is the Middle East's biggest IT infrastructure, is built inside a free trade zone, and has the largest commercial Internet Protocol Telephony system in the world.

Dubai Internet City is a strategic base for companies targeting emerging markets in the vast region extending from the Middle East to the Indian subcontinent and Africa—a region covering 2 billion people with a GDP of $ 6.7 trillion. It's in Dubai where you'll find Arab investors who have pulled billions of dollars out of Western financial markets meeting with Indians and the Chinese to relocate their investments to these new markets.

In line with Dubai's liberal economic policies and regulations, Dubai Internet City offers foreign companies 100% tax-free ownership, 100% repatriation of capital and profits, no currency restrictions, easy registration and licensing, stringent cyber regulations, and protection of intellectual property. The global ICT giants are all there: Microsoft, Oracle, HP, IBM, Compaq, Dell, Siemens, Canon, Logica, Sony, Ericsson and Cisco, to name just a few. The cluster of ICT companies in Dubai Internet City is comprised of software development, business services, e-commerce, consultancy, education and training, sales and marketing, and back office operations. DIC provides a scalable state-of-the-art technology platform that allows companies looking to provide cost effective business process outsourcing (BPO) services such as call center operations."[19]

Not bad for a Arab dark alley, eh?

Friedman especially likes to bash Saudi Arabia, "Think about the whole mind-set of bin Ladenism. It is to 'purge' Saudi Arabia of all foreigners and foreign influences. That is exactly the opposite of glocalizing and collaborating. Tribal culture and thinking still dominate in many Arab countries, and the tribal mind-set is also anathema to collaboration." It seems Friedman is confused, for it was Saudi Arabia that purged Osama bin Laden from Saudi Arabia. The Arab street where Friedman says the elite don't invest is indeed a prime example of Friedman's glocalization. It seems Friedman has the same confused thinking about tribal friction as he does about nation-state friction as an impediment to his simplistic view of the emergence of a global market—a worldwide system of production and consumption that disregards national and cultural boundaries.

As a contributor to the book, *Extreme Competition,* American expatriate, Omar Ragel, paints a picture far different from Friedman's. Ragel explains the current investment situation in the Gulf states, "Recent political threats, and the imposition of a massive regime of investment restrictions by the current U.S. administration, has seen billions of dollars pulled out of Western financial markets and brought home, where it has found a bright, creative and energetic twenty-first century business environment."

Then, of course, there's Friedman's neologism about "Reform Retail," where only developing countries that "get it" will become part of Friedman's flat world, "It involves looking at four key aspects of your society—infrastructure, regulatory institutions, education, and culture (the general way your country and leaders relate to the world)—and upgrading each one to remove as many friction points as possible. The idea of reform retail is to enable the greatest number of your people to have the best legal and institutional framework within which to innovate, start companies, and become attractive partners for those who want to collaborate with them from elsewhere in the world." Once again, down those dark alleys that Friedman claims makes up the Arab world, you just might stumble upon the Carnegie Mellon campus in Qatar. Not only does Qatar have a world-class infrastructure, it has invested in world-class education, both of which are examples of Friedman's reform retail.

Let's now go with Friedman and turn our attention to what he describes as another loser in this new flat world, Mexico. Friedman explains Mexico's dismal economic development failure after the advent of NAFTA to be due to a lack of "Reform Retail." There is, however, another perspective, one expressed by Nobel-prize winning economist, Joseph Stiglitz., "One of the reasons that Mexico fared poorly in competition with China was that China was investing heavily in infrastructure and education. Mexico's limited tax revenue, exacerbated by the loss of tariff revenue [as a result of NAFTA], was one reason why it did not make the necessary investments.

"NAFTA was not really a free trade agreement. America retained its agriculture subsidies. NAFTA pitted the heavily subsidized U.S. agribusiness sector against peasant producers and family farms in Mexico. U.S. farmers export many of their products into Mexico at costs far below those of the local market, driving down prices for local farmers. America also continued to use what were effectively non-tariff barriers to keep out some of Mexico's products.

"These policies hurt rural livelihoods. One-fifth of Mexico's workers are employed in the agricultural sector, and 75 percent of Mexico's poverty is found in rural areas. While some large Mexican agribusiness sectors have expanded their exports, much of Mexico's rural sector is in crisis. Local farms are threatened by cheap imports from the United States, falling commodity prices and reduced government support. Four-fifths of the population of rural Mexico lives in poverty, and more than half are in extreme poverty."[20]

Friedman simply ignores the historical facts that Stiglitz describes. "None of today's rich countries developed by simply opening themselves to foreign trade. All the developed countries used a wide range of trade policy instruments, a fact that should make their WTO ambassadors blush when they sit down to negotiate with today's developing countries. China and India provide two examples. Both have successfully integrated into the world trading system, and both have benefited greatly from international trade, yet neither followed orthodox trade liberalization policies. China has been particularly careful to ensure that its economic development strategy is gradually implemented and carefully sequenced. China has become more open in recent years, and has benefited from doing so, but trade liberalization did not cause China's growth. China began to grow rapidly in the late 1970s, but trade liberalization did not start until the late 1980s, and only took off in the 1990s, long after the country had demonstrated its ability to sustain strong economic growth." This is quite the opposite from the path imposed on Mexico with the advent of NAFTA.

Friedman paints a picture of Mexico not being able to compete with China as a result of what he ascribes as "intangibles." Friedman writes, "And in Mexico City, just when Mexicans thought they had turned the corner forever, they ran smack into China, coming the other way and running much faster. What explains these differences?

We know the basic formula for economic success—reform wholesale, followed by reform retail, plus good governance, education, infrastructure, and the ability to glocalize. What we don't know, though, and what I would bottle and sell if I did, is the answer to the question of why one country gets its act together to do all these things in a sustained manner and why another one doesn't. India and China both have a long tradition of parents telling their children that the greatest thing they can be in life is an engineer or a doctor. But building the schools to make that happen in Mexico simply has not been done. India and China each have more than fifty thousand students studying in the United States today. They come from about twelve time zones away. Mexico, which is smaller but right next door, has only about ten thousand." Friedman goes on to summarize Mexico's state of affairs, "In other words, it's reform retail, stupid."

NAFTA, unfortunately, flattened Mexico's tax base. To paraphrase Friedman, "It takes money to build schools, stupid."

In short, Friedman's assertions regarding "Wholesale and Retail Reform" are superficial, and they ignore the fundamental issues of free and *fair* trade.

Part 4: Companies and the Flat World

Chapter 11: How Companies Cope

Wikipedia: Friedman offers seven rules for companies aspiring to be successful in the era of "Globalization 3.0."

1.) When the world goes flat, and you are feeling flattened, reach for a shovel and dig inside yourself. Don't try to build walls.

2.) One way small companies flourish in the flat world is by learning to act really big. And the key to being small and acting big is being quick to take advantage of all the new tools for collaboration to reach farther, faster, wider, and deeper.

3.) One way that big companies learn to flourish in the flat world is by learning how to act really small by enabling their customers to act really big.

4.) The best companies are the best collaborators. In the flat world, more business will be done through collaborations within and between companies, for a few simple reasons: The next layers of value creation, whether in technology, marketing, biomedicine, or manufacturing, are becoming so complex that no single firm or department is going to be able to master them alone.

5.) In a flat world, the best companies stay healthy by getting regular chest X-rays and then selling the results to their clients. To constantly identify and strengthen their niches, and outsource the stuff that is not very differentiating.

6.) The best companies outsource to win, not to shrink. They outsource to innovate faster and more cheaply in order to grow larger, gain market share, and hire more and different specialists, not to save money by firing more people.

7.) Outsourcing isn't just for Benedict Arnolds. It's also for idealists. To make a positive impact on the world, it is better to teach someone to fish vs. just giving him a fish.

As Friedman says, "I am not a business writer and this is not a how-to-succeed-in-business book." So one wonders why he wrote the chapter at all, other than to achieve some sort of page count for the book.

Here's the core of his message, "As I conducted interviews for this book, I kept hearing the same phrase from different business executives. It was strange; they all used it, as if they had all been talking to each other. The phrase was, 'Just in the last couple of years...' Time and again, entrepreneurs and innovators from all different types of businesses, large and small, told me that 'just in the last couple of years' they had been able to do things they had never dreamed possible before, or that they were being forced to do things they had never dreamed necessary before.

"I am convinced that these entrepreneurs and CEOs were responding to the triple convergence. Each was figuring out a strategy for his or her company to thrive or at least survive in this new environment. Just as individuals need a strategy for coping with the flattening of the world, so too do companies. My economics tutor Paul Romer is fond of saying, 'Everyone wants economic growth, but nobody wants change.' Unfortunately, you cannot have one without the other, especially when the playing field shifts as dramatically as it has since the year 2000. If you want to grow and flourish in a flat world, you better learn how to change and align yourself with it."

Friedman contacts his corporate CEO network to discover and, then, to reveal to us what he considers breakthroughs for the twenty-first century, "Howard Schultz, the founder and chairman of Starbucks, says that Starbucks estimates that it is possible to make nineteen thousand variations of coffee on the basis of the menus posted at any Starbucks outlet. What Starbucks did, in other words, was make its customers its drink designers and allow them to customize their drinks to their exact specifications. Starbucks never thought of offering soy milk, Schultz told me, until store managers started to get bombarded with demands for it from customers, to the point where they were going to the grocery store across the street in the middle of the day to buy cartons of soy milk. Starbucks learned from its customers, and today some 8 percent of all the drinks that Starbucks sells include soy milk. 'We didn't dream up the different concoctions with soy milk,' said Schultz, 'the customers did.' Starbucks just collaborated with them. The smartest big companies clearly understand that the triple convergence allows them to collaborate with their customers in a totally new fashion—and, by doing so, to act really small. The way that big companies act small is not by targeting each individual consumer and trying to serve that customer individually. That would be impossible and impossibly expensive. They do it by making their business, as much as possible, into a buffet.

"These companies create a platform that allows individual customers to serve themselves in their own way, at their own pace, in their own time, according to their own tastes. They are actually making their customers their employees and having them pay the company for that pleasure at the same time!"

This brilliant new business idea has a name, "prosumer," and it was introduced over thirty years ago, long before the world supposedly went flat. Prosumer is a contraction of producer and consumer. In 1972, Marshall McLuhan and Barrington Nevitt suggested that, with electric technology, the consumer would become a producer. In 1980, futurologist Alvin Toffler, coined the term when he predicted that the role of producers and consumers would begin to merge and blur.

If you are in business and want to understand how to stay relevant in Friedman's supposed flat world, you'll have to look elsewhere, for you'll find nothing new in his flat book.

Part 5: Geopolitics and the Flat World

Chapter 12: The Unflat World

Wikipedia: Friedman discusses his philosophy of history: "I am a technological determinist! ... I believe that capabilities create intentions. ... But ... I am not a historical determinist." He admits that he has exaggerated many of the features of the contemporary world that he has been describing, and notes: "I know that the world is not flat." "Middle class" is, according to Friedman, a state of mind and a key to social stability. He praises the Bill and Melinda Gates Foundation for looking out for, in Bill Gates' words, "that other 3 billion." Friedman briefly notes the existence of the "half flat": rural India, rural China, rural Eastern Europe. He claims to identify the five forces that drive the anti-globalization movement: liberal guilt, rearguard socialism, nostalgia, anti-Americanism, and criticism of process, and castigates all but the last of these. Once again he tries to diagnose the frustration and humiliation of Arab-Muslim cultures, and offers this prescription: self-realization and confession. China's embrace of automobile culture is critiqued.

Not every country has or at this point can gain from the flat world (these countries are either "unflat" or "caught in the middle.")

Reasons that flatness will not spread to some include: Too Sick, Too Disempowered, Too Frustrated (negative influence of humiliation), Too many Toyotas (perils of rising middle class).

Friedman opens "The Unflat World" with a confession, "... ever since I began writing about globalization, I've been challenged by critics along one particular line: 'Isn't there a certain technological determinism to your argument? To listen to you, Friedman, there are these ten flatteners, they are converging and flattening the earth, and there is nothing that people can do but bow to them and join the parade. And after a transition, everyone will get richer and smarter and it will all be fine. But you're wrong, because the history of the world suggests that ideological alternatives, and power alternatives, have always arisen to any system, and globalization will be no different.' This is a legitimate question, so let me try to answer it directly: *I am a technological determinist! Guilty as charged.* [The italics are his.]

"I believe that capabilities create intentions. If we create an Internet where people can open an online store and have global suppliers, global customers, and global competitors, they will open that online store or bank or bookshop. If we create work flow platforms that allow companies to disaggregate any job and source it to the knowledge center anywhere in the world that can perform that task most efficiently at the lowest cost, companies will do that sort of outsourcing. If we create cell phones with cameras in them, people will use them for all sorts of tasks, from cheating on tests to calling Grandma in her nursing home on her ninetieth birthday from the top of a mountain in New Zealand. The history of economic development teaches this over and over: If you can do it, you must do it, otherwise your competitors will—and as this book has tried to demonstrate, there is a whole new universe of things that companies, countries, and individuals can and must do to thrive in a flat world. But while I am a technological determinist, I am not a historical determinist. There is absolutely no guarantee that everyone will use these new technologies, or the triple convergence, for the benefit of themselves, their countries, or humanity. These are just technologies. Using them does not make you modern, smart, moral, wise, fair, or decent. It just makes you able to communicate, compete, and collaborate farther and faster. In the absence of a world-destabilizing war, every one of these technologies will become cheaper, lighter, smaller and more personal, mobile, digital, and virtual. Therefore, more and more people will find more and more ways to use them. We can only hope that more people in more places will use them to create, collaborate, and grow their living standards, not the opposite. But it doesn't have to happen. To put it another way, I don't know how the flattening of the world will come out.

"Indeed, this is the point in the book where I have to make a confession: I know that the world is not flat.

"Yes, you read me right: *I know that the world is not flat.* Don't worry. I know."

"I am certain, though, that the world has been shrinking and flattening for some time now, and that process has quickened dramatically in recent years. Half the world today is directly or indirectly participating in the flattening process or feeling its effects. I have engaged in literary license in titling this book *The World Is Flat* to draw attention to this flattening and its quickening pace because I think it is the single most important trend in the world today."

There is a lot to digest in this excerpt from "The Unflat World." John Gray of the London School of Economics provides this analysis, "Friedman has emerged as the most powerful contemporary publicist of neoliberal ideas. Neoliberals have a wide variety of views on political and social matters, ranging from the highly conservative standpoint of Friedrich Hayek to the more rigorously libertarian position of Milton Friedman; but they are at one in seeing the free market as the fountainhead of human freedom. Though in some of his writings he shows a concern for the casualties of deregulated markets, Thomas Friedman is a passionate missionary for this neoliberal faith. In his view the free market brings with it most of the ingredients that make for a free and humanly fulfilling society, and he has propagated this creed indefatigably in his books and in columns in *The New York Times.* ". . . it may be instructive to note the matters in which he shares Marx's blind spots. Because they were on opposite sides of the cold war it is often assumed that neoliberalism and Marxism are fundamentally antagonistic systems of ideas. In fact they belong to the same style of thinking, and share many of the same disabling limitations. For Marxists and neoliberals alike it is technological advance that fuels economic development, and economic forces that shape society. Politics and culture are secondary phenomena, sometimes capable of retarding human progress; but in the last analysis they cannot prevail against advancing technology and growing productivity.

"Friedman is unequivocal in endorsing this reductive philosophy. He writes that he is often asked if he is a technological determinist, and with the innocent enthusiasm that is a redeeming feature of his prose style he declares resoundingly: 'This is a legitimate question, so let me try to answer it directly: *I am a technological determinist! Guilty as charged.*'

"Technological determinism may contain a kernel of truth but it suggests a misleadingly simple view of history. This is well illustrated in Friedman's account of the demise of the Soviet Union. Acknowledging that there 'was no single cause,' he goes on: 'To some degree the termites just ate away at the foundations of the Soviet Union, which were already weakened by the system's own internal contradictions and inefficiencies; to some degree the Reagan administration's military buildup in Europe forced the Kremlin to bankrupt itself paying for warheads; and to some degree Mikhail Gorbachev's hapless efforts to reform something that was unreformable brought communism to an end. But if I had to point to one factor as first among equals, it was the information revolution that began in the early- to mid-1980s. Totalitarian systems depend on a monopoly of information and force, and too much information started to slip through the

Iron Curtain, thanks to the spread of fax machines, telephones, and other modern tools of communication.'

"What is striking in this otherwise unexceptionable list is what it leaves out. There is no mention of the role of Solidarity and the Catholic Church in making Poland the first post-Communist country, or of the powerful independence movements that developed in the Baltic nations during the Eighties. Most strikingly, there is no mention of the [Soviet Union's] war in Afghanistan. By any account strategic defeat at the hands of Western-armed Islamist forces in that country (including some that formed the organization which was later to become al-Qaeda) was a defining moment in the decline of Soviet power. If Friedman ignores these events, it may be because they attest to the persistent power of religion and nationalism— forces that in his simple, deterministic worldview should be withering away.

"It is an irony of history that a view of the world falsified by the Communist collapse should have been adopted, in some of its most misleading aspects, by the victors in the cold war. Neoliberals, such as Friedman, have reproduced the weakest features of Marx's thought—its consistent underestimation of nationalist and religious movements and its unidirectional view of history. They have failed to absorb Marx's insights into the anarchic and self-destructive qualities of capitalism. Marx viewed the unfettered market as a revolutionary force, and understood that its expansion throughout the world was bound to be disruptive and violent. As capitalism spreads, it turns society upside down, destroying entire industries, ways of life, and regimes. This can hardly be expected to be a peaceful process, and in fact it has been accompanied by major conflicts and social upheavals. The expansion of European capitalism in the nineteenth century involved the Opium Wars, genocide in the Belgian Congo, the Great Game in Central Asia, and many other forms of imperial conquest and rivalry. The seeming triumph of global capitalism at the end of the twentieth century followed two world wars, the cold war, and savage neocolonial conflicts.

"Over the past two hundred years, the spread of capitalism and industrialization has gone hand in hand with war and revolution. It is a fact that would not have surprised Marx. Why do Friedman and other neoliberals believe things will be any different in the twenty-first century? Part of the answer lies in an ambiguity in the idea of globalization. In current discussion two different notions are commonly conflated: the belief that we are living in a period of rapid and continuous technological innovation, which has the effect of linking up events and activities throughout the world more widely and quickly than before; and the belief that this process is leading to a single worldwide economic system. The first is an empirical proposition and plainly true, the second a groundless ideological assertion. Like Marx, Friedman elides the two."[21]

Let's look at Friedman's numbers, "I am certain, though, that the world has been shrinking and flattening for some time now, and that process has quickened dramatically in recent years. Half the world today is directly or indirectly participating in the flattening process or feeling its effects." If half the world today is directly or indirectly participating in the flattening process or feeling its effects, that would be about 3 billion people. Let's look at just India, Friedman's shining star in a flat world. As Alexander Cockburn reminds us in, "Thomas Friedman's Imaginary World," "Remember, India has a billion people in it. Maybe 2 percent of them get to fly in a plane or go online."[22] Looking at such numbers, it's tough to support the assertion that half the world's 6.5 billion people are ready to plug and play into Friedman's imaginary flat-world platform.

Cockburn goes on to describe Friedman's neoliberal reaction to the rejection of an European Union constitution, "It was striking how many [neoliberal journalists], presumably without any direct orders from the owners of their publications, started lecturing the French in the tones of nineteenth-century Masters of Capital. The 'Non,' they howled, disclosed the cosseted and selfish laziness of French workers. On inspection this turned out to mean that French workers have laws protecting their pensions, health benefits, leisure time and other outlandish buttresses of a tolerable existence. No one was more outraged than Friedman, a man who, we can safely surmise, does have health benefits, enjoys confidence about his retirement along with a robust six-figure income plus guaranteed vacations plus a pleasant ambulatory existence living in nice hotels, confabbing with CEOs, and lecturing gratified businessmen on their visionary nature and the virtues of selfishness.

"From Bangalore, Friedman issued a furious rebuke. 'French voters are trying to preserve a 35-hour work week in a world where Indian engineers are ready to work a 35-hour day. Next to India, Western Europe looks like an assisted-living facility with Turkish nurses.' I guess it does, though 'engineers' is rather a dignified label to fix on the cyber-coolies—underpaid clerical workers—who toil night and day in Bangalore's call centers. But if you want a race to the bottom of the sort Friedman calls for, you don't have to travel too far from Bangalore, maybe—though any direction will do—north-east into the former realm of poster boy Naidu [CEO of Infosys] to find an Indian reality compared with which the so-called IT breakthroughs in India are like gnat bites on the hide of one of those buffaloes you see in photos in articles headlined 'Timeless India Faces Change.'

"In the Naidu years at least 5,000 Indian farmers committed suicide. Across India, they're still killing themselves. (A Kisan Sabha farmers' union survey of just 26 households in Wayanad, in northern Kerala, that had seen suicides shows a total debt of over Rs. 2 million. Or about Rs. 82,000 per household, which is the equivalent of just under $2,000. The average size of these farms is less than 1.4 acres. And a good chunk of that debt is owed to private lenders.)"

Friedman goes on to describe the ultimate goal of his flat world: attaining entry into some sort of global middle class.

"I once heard Jerry Yang, the cofounder of Yahoo!, quote a senior Chinese government official as saying, 'Where people have hope, you have a middle class.' I think this is a very useful insight. The existence of large, stable middle classes around the world is crucial to geopolitical stability, but middle class is a state of mind, not a state of income. That's why a majority of Americans always describe themselves as 'middle class,' even though by income statistics some of them wouldn't be considered as such. 'Middle class' is another way of describing people who believe that they have a pathway out of poverty or lower-income status toward a higher standard of living and a better future for their kids. *You can be in the middle class in your head whether you make $2 a day or $200, if you believe in social mobility—that your kids have a chance to live better than you do—and that hard work and playing by the rules of your society will get you where you want to go.* [italics ours] In many ways, the line between those who are in the flat world and those who are not is this line of hope."

So, all you need is $2 a day to be in the middle class! This globalization stuff is nothing less than magic. But wait just a minute. Earlier, you had to plug and play into Friedman's mythical platform and collaborate horizontally to join the flatheads. Now you just have to have hope. How does Friedman cope with the problems impeding his flattening process, and how might we collaborate better to overcome them? He lists four key obstacles: Too Sick, Too Disempowered, Too Frustrated (negative influence of humiliation), and Too many Toyotas (perils of rising middle class).

Here's his corporate exemplar for Too Sick, "... there are many,

many others living outside this cycle. They live in villages or rural areas that only criminals would want to invest in, regions where violence, civil war, and disease compete with one another to see which can ravage the civilian population most. The world will be entirely flat only when all these people are brought into it. One of the few people with enough dollars to make a difference who has stepped up to this challenge is Microsoft chairman Bill Gates, whose $27 billion Bill and Melinda Gates Foundation has focused on this huge, disease-ravaged, opportunity-deprived population."

Friedman goes on, "Let's stop here for a moment and imagine how beneficial it would be for the world, and for America, if rural China, India, and Africa were to grow into little Americas or European Unions in economic and opportunity terms. But the chances of their getting into such a virtuous cycle is tiny without a real humanitarian push by flat-world businesses, philanthropies, and governments to devote more resources to their problems. The only way out is through new ways of collaboration between the flat and unflat parts of the world."

It's that collaboration thing again. When did businesses ever put "humanitarian push" in their corporate mission statements? Reading *The Corporation: The Pathological Pursuit of Profit and Power,* by Joel Bakan, will help you learn just what makes corporation tick, what motivates them, and what they are chartered to do. They are not evil, but their missions are to increase stockholder value, not to provide humanitarian push. A corporation's charter is to make money, and Wall Street will accept nothing less!

Free-trade evangelist, Jagdish Bhagwati, writes in his book, *In Defense of Globalization,* "If multinationals avoid some poor countries, that is surely not surprising. They are businesses that must survive by making a profit. If a country wants to attract investment, it has to provide an attractive environment. That generally implies having political stability and economic advantages such as cheap labor or exploitable natural labor."

Moving from Bill Gates' philanthropy to save those who are Too Sick, Friedman turns his attention to the Too Disempowered. Friedman's view, through his own rose-colored glasses, colors his understanding of the implications of what he is reporting. By his own admission, "As exciting and as visible as the flat Indian high-tech sector is, have no illusions: It accounts for 0.2 percent of employment in India. Add those Indians involved in manufacturing for export, and you get a total of 2 percent of employment in India. The half flat are all those other hundreds of millions of people, particularly in rural India, rural China, and rural Eastern Europe, who are close enough to see, touch, and occasionally benefit from the flat world but who are not really living inside it themselves."

This means that of India's 1 billion people, only 2 million can plug and play in the high-tech sector of his flat world. Let's see, 1 billion minus 2 million equals 998 million people left out of Friedman's golden country of laissez-faire corporate globalization. It must be that selling millions of books is more important than accurately reporting about the hundreds of millions left-behind (the half flat, as Friedman calls them) Indians, many of whom are being flattened by unfair trade agreements.

Regardless of the numbers, neoliberal Friedman seems to suspect the true cause of these left behind people is those darn "global populists," and their lack of horizontal collaboration. "How can outsiders collaborate in this process? I think, first and foremost, they can redefine the meaning of global populism. If populists really want to help the rural poor, the way to do it is not by burning down McDonald's and shutting down the IMF and trying to put up protectionist barriers that will unflatten the world. That will help the rural poor not one iota. It has to be by refocusing the energies of the global populist movement on how to improve local government, infrastructure, and education in places like rural India and China, so the populations there can acquire the tools to collaborate and participate in the flat world. The global populist movement, better known as the antiglobalization movement, has a great deal of energy, but up to now it has been too divided and confused to effectively help the poor in any meaningful or sustained manner. It needs a policy lobotomy."

Hmm, wasn't the universal spread of corporate globalism, combined with Bill and Melinda Gates' philanthropy, supposed to save the world? Now, is it up to those "global populists," but we cannot rely upon them until they first get a policy lobotomy.

After all, how are all these impoverished people going to have a McDonald's and a Wal-Mart if these global populists keep nipping at the heals of unfettered, deregulated free-market, neoliberal, corporate globalizers? Friedman concludes, "What the world doesn't need now is for the antiglobalization movement to go away. We just need it to grow up."

Okay, let's move on to Too Frustrated, where Friedman returns to one of is favorite subjects, demonizing the Arab-Muslim world. He continues his worries about Islamo-Leninists and bin Ladenisms that converted Islam into a political ideology of religious totalitarianism. They want to install the reign of perfect religion, while Friedman wants to install the reign of perfect neoliberalism.

This debate could get nasty, so we just won't go there in this little book. Don't we all already know, as Friedman reminds us, that "...the problem is that so many Muslims want both stagnation and power: they want a return to the perfection of the seventh century and to dominate the twenty-first, as they believe is the birthright of their doctrine, the last testament of God to man." We'll just leave it at that and recognize that it's that evil versus good thing.

Finally, Friedman gets to a very important impediment to his utopian flat world, Too Many Toyotas. We are happy to agree with him when he's right, and here we fully agree that "... another barrier to the flattening of the world is emerging, one that is not a human constraint but a natural resource constraint. If millions of people from India, China, Latin America, and the former Soviet Empire who were living largely outside the flat world all start to walk onto the flat world playing field at once—and all come with their own dream of owning a car, a house, a refrigerator, a microwave, and a toaster—we are going to experience either a serious energy shortage or, worse, wars over energy that would have a profoundly unflattening effect on the world. At worst, we are going to set off a global struggle for natural resources and junk up, heat up, garbage up, smoke up and devour our little planet faster than at any time in the history of the planet. Be afraid, I certainly am."

In the first edition of his book, Friedman concludes this section with "I would love to see a grand, China-United States Manhattan Project, a crash program to jointly develop clean alternative energies, bringing together China's best scientists and its political ability to implement pilot projects, with America's best brains, technology, and money. It would be the ideal model and the ideal project for creating value horizontally, with each side contributing its strength." In the second edition it's "Enough of this nonsense that conservation, energy efficiency, and environmentalism are some hobby we cannot afford. I can't think of anything more cowardly or un-American. Real patriots, real advocates of spreading democracy around the world, live green. Green is the new red white and blue."

Now, there's a nice poetic revision that will surely play well on his speaking circuit. But providing so little discussion on this critical obstacle to his flat world is a real disappointment. Oh well, now that Friedman has a shiny new SUV, as reported by *Fortune* magazine, let's just leave it at that and say, as his section title observed, there are, indeed, Too Many Toyotas.

Chapter 13: Globalization and the Local

In this new second-edition chapter, Friedman announces that "… the cultural revolution is about to begin. … Indeed it is becoming clear that the flat-world platform, while it has the potential to homogenize cultures, also has, I would argue, an even greater potential to nourish diversity to a degree the world has never seen before.

"Why? Primarily because of uploading…. The newest anti-homogenizing force is podcasting—a whole new tool for globalizing the local…. because the ease of uploading and podcasting means there are almost no barriers to entry, as long as you have a computer, a camera, and a microphone."

Remember that Friedman says that only 0.2 percent of India's population has high-tech employment. Or consider that, in 2004, there were 87 million people online in mainland China and 31.1 million had broadband access, according to China Internet Network Information Center (CCNIC, July 2004). Now, we don't have statistics on how many of those 31.1 million have cameras and microphones, but even if they all did, only 0.3 percent of Chinese and 0.2 percent of Indians have a chance to upload and podcast to preserve their culture as corporate globalization flattens the cultures of the remaining 99.97+% that cannot reach Friedman's utopian platform. Oh well. Marie Antoinette is famous for, "If they have no bread, then let them eat cake!" The equivalent neoliberal quote for the masses might be, "If they are worried about their culture, let them podcast!"

According to an April 2005 report by the Human Rights Watch,[23] "China is known for tight constraints on freedom of religion. This is particularly evident in its northwest Xinjiang Uighur Autonomous Region (XUAR), an *oil-rich area* that borders eight other nations. Here the Muslim Uighurs, the largest non-Chinese ethnic group in the region, are under wholesale assault by the state. Since September 11, 2001, China has attempted to position its repression of Uighurs as part of the global war on terror. China has opportunistically used the post-September 11 environment to make the outrageous claim that individuals disseminating peaceful religious and cultural messages in Xinjiang are terrorists who have simply changed tactics. For most Uighurs the paramount issue is not religion per se but the perceived threat that religious repression poses to their distinct identity coupled with their acute feeling of being colonized. [The Uighur region is oil rich, and the Chinese are building railroads and roads to bring in a new Chinese population to exploit that oil.] They view the tight restrictions placed by the Chinese authorities on Uighur Islam as an attempt to debase their very identity, as Islam is an essential component of their traditional identity and culture."

Fortunately, there is a solution for the Uighurs; they can follow Friedman's advice and use iPods to maintain their culture, their religion, and their identity. That should not be too difficult as iPods are assembled in China. On June 11, 2006, the *Mail*, a U.K. newspaper published the report, "iPod City." It offers a rare glimpse inside Apple's massive iPod manufacturing facilities, which are owned by Foxconn. Its exterior gates flaunt billboards encouraging anyone over the age of 16 to apply for a job. Inside Foxconn's Longhua facility, workers labor 15 hours a day building iPods, for which they usually earn about $50 per month. When they're not on the assembly lines, they live in secluded dormitories that each house 100 people and prohibit visitors from the outside world. The workers are allowed "a few possessions" and a "bucket to wash their clothes." "We have to work too hard and I am always tired. It's like being in the army," Zang Lan, one of the workers at Longhua, told the *Mail*. "They make us stand still for hours. If we move we are punished by being made to stand still for longer. The boys are made to do pushups."[24]

Friedman concludes his globalization of the local, and of the newest anti-homogenizing force, in China, "And you thought the Cultural Revolution was over. Sorry, it's just beginning. Only China's newest Cultural Revolution is going to be driven this time from the bottom up—thanks to the flat-world platform—by podcasters with Apple's little white iPods, not from the top down by Maoists with Little Red Books."

To paraphrase Professor Frankfurt, that's pure bullshit. And don't forget that Friedman also ignores the censorship rules to which

Microsoft, Yahoo! and Google must adhere in China.

Chapter 14: The Dell Theory of Conflict Prevention

Wikipedia: With the help of Dell, Inc., Friedman describes in detail the history of the Dell laptop on which this book was written. This serves as an introduction to the importance of just-in-time supply chains as an influence on international relations. "[T]he advent and spread of just-in-time global supply chains in the flat world are an even greater restraint on geopolitical adventurism than the more general rising standard of living that McDonald's symbolized [in Friedman's book The Lexus and the Olive Tree].... Because people embedded in major global supply chains don't want to fight old-time wars anymore." Supply-chain membership is an asset that national elites are wary of risking in war. Crises with Taiwan and China, and between India and Pakistan are presented as successful test cases of Friedman's "Dell theory of conflict prevention." Friedman discusses Al-Qaeda as an exploiter of flat-world technology, forming "mutant global supply chains," and cites the report by Gabriel Weimann of Haifa University on terrorists' use of the Internet. In discussing nuclear terrorism, Friedman endorses Graham Allison's "doctrine of the Three No's: No loose nukes, No new nascent nukes, and No new nuclear states." But the similarity of the Internet to the Tower of Babel is denied.

In this chapter, Friedman is now ready to explain how to end war. In his last book, it was up to McDonald's to stamp out war, in this one it's Dell. Friedman writes, "In *The Lexus and the Olive Tree* I argued that to the extent that countries tied their economies and futures to global integration and trade, it would act as a restraint on going to war with their neighbors. I first started thinking about this in the late 1990s, when, during my travels, I noticed that no two countries that both had McDonald's had ever fought a war against each other since each got its McDonald's. (Border skirmishes and civil wars don't count, because McDonald's usually served both sides.) After confirming this with McDonald's, I offered what I called the Golden Arches Theory of Conflict Prevention. The Golden Arches Theory stipulated that when a country reached the level of economic development where it had a middle class big enough to support a network of McDonald's, it became a McDonald's country. And people in McDonald's countries didn't like to fight wars anymore. They preferred to wait in line for burgers."

Oops. NATO bombed Serbia, and both Serbia and most, if not all, NATO member states have at least one McDonald's.

It seems Friedman forgot to stick by his earlier writings that "The hidden hand of the market will never work without a hidden fist— McDonald's cannot flourish without McDonnell Douglas, the builder of the F-15."[25] Doesn't this mean open world markets are kept open by force of arms?

Since the Golden Arches Theory did not hold true, Friedman needed a new savior of world peace in *The World is Flat*. Let's see, let me try Dell "... and again with tongue slightly in cheek, I offer the Dell Theory of Conflict Prevention. [Is tongue-in-cheek an appropriate way to talk about war?] The Dell Theory stipulates: No two countries that are both part of a major global supply chain, like Dell's, will ever fight a war against each other as long as they are both part of the same global supply chain. Because people embedded in major global supply chains don't want to fight old-time wars anymore. They want to make just-in-time deliveries of goods and services— and enjoy the rising standards of living that come with that."

It sound like a fine theory, but wait, Friedman is about to take back what he just said, just like he did in the last chapter when he confessed the he knows that the world is not flat, "Warning: What I said when I put forth the McDonald's theory, I would repeat even more strenuously with the Dell Theory: It does not make wars obsolete. And it does not guarantee that governments will not engage in wars of choice, even governments that are part of major supply chains. To suggest so would be *naïve*.

"It guarantees only that governments whose countries are enmeshed in global supply chains will have to think three times, not just twice, about engaging in anything but a war of self-defense. And if they choose to go to war anyway, the price they will pay will be ten times higher than it was a decade ago and probably ten times higher than whatever the leaders of that country think. It is one thing to lose your McDonald's. It's quite another to fight a war that costs you your place in a twenty-first–century supply chain that may not come back around for a long time."

How does he support the assertion that "governments whose countries are enmeshed in global supply chains will have to think *three* [emphasis added] times, not just *twice* ... [and] the price they will pay will be *ten* times higher than it was a decade ago and probably ten times higher than whatever the leaders of that country think."? On what basis does Friedman conclude that counties will have to think three times before starting a conflict and that its cost will be ten times higher than a decade ago? If Friedman is to continue shaping the policies of world leaders, some documented facts would serve him better than simply saying, "never mind, I didn't really mean that, it was only tongue slightly in cheek."

Friedman continues, "Obviously, since Iraq, Syria, south Lebanon, North Korea, Pakistan, Afghanistan, and Iran are not part of any major global supply chains, all of them remain hot spots that could explode at any time and slow or reverse the flattening of the world."

What? Iraq used to be a part of one of the world's most vital petroleum supply chains, but has since been flattened and turned into a very dark alley by a preemptive war. Since Iran is a major component of China's energy supply chain, why is Iran on Friedman's list of hot spots since it, too, is part of a major global supply chain? And Afghanistan is the key supplier of poppy products to the U.S., which, once again, is part of a major global supply chain. Why are they on the list? Why aren't Sudan, Somalia, Rwanda and Yemen on the list? Is it because they have no supply chains, or is it that the one-world, free-market neoliberals don't consider them to be worthy of thought or consideration?

Friedman describes the Internet as a two-edged sword that can be used by Al-Qaeda as well as by free-market capitalists. Is this some new insight? Don't we all know that technology always presents humankind with a two-edge sword? It was Isaac Asimov who, in the 1970s, argued that modern medicine was the technology that would most likely wipe out mankind. He argued that it was the discovery of the microscope that led to the germ theory of disease and laid the foundation for modern medicine. Now, instead of two out of nine children of rural families surviving, eight do. The world population has grown ever since, from 978 million in 1800 to 6.5 billion in 2006, and will be an estimated 9 billion in 2050. Indeed, the Internet can be used for the good of mankind, or it can be used to its detriment. Ditto for modern medicine.

Furthermore, Al-Qaeda, or any other well funded terrorist group, or insurgents, insurrectionists, malcontents, mutineers, nihilists, rebels, revolters, or revolutionaries could wipe out Wall Street and paralyze the world economy with a suitcase bomb *without* the assistance of the Internet. Or they could use modern medicine to launch a biological bomb without first launching a Web site. In an earlier era, Friedman's Infosys versus Al-Qaeda argument would probably have focused on the satellite revolution, as satellite communications was the hot new technology. Shutting down the Internet as one means of shutting off Al-Qaeda's "suicide supply chain," as Friedman calls it, is irrelevant, even if Friedman thinks that it's impossible without also undermining ourselves. There is enough nasty stuff in hospital radiology trash bins and former Soviet dumping grounds to do the trick. And tribal channels of communication do just fine for getting the poppy crop from Afghanistan to the streets of New York City. Perhaps a couple of disposable cell phones purchased from a convenience store could turbocharge that supply chain.

Friedman pulls the disparate ideas in this chapter together by asking his religious teacher, Rabbi Tzvi Marx from Holland, if he sees the Internet as a heresy. "Absolutely not," said Marx. "The heresy is not that mankind works together—it is to what ends. It is essential that we use this new ability to communicate and collaborate for the right ends—for constructive human aims and not megalomaniacal ends. Building a tower [referring to the Tower of Babel] was megalomaniacal. Bin Laden's insistence that he has the truth and can flatten anyone else's tower who doesn't heed him is megalomaniacal. Collaborating so mankind can achieve its full potential is God's hope."

Although there is much doubt about the link between Saddam Hussain and Al-Qaeda, Friedman has strong convictions about the link between Al-Qaeda and the Internet. Should we indeed make a preemptive strike against the Internet? After all, Friedman paints the picture that Al-Qaeda couldn't function without the support of the Internet. Is the Internet heresy, or a weapon of mass destruction? This discussion is, you know, more bullshit.

Part 6: Conclusion: Imagination

Chapter 15: 11/9 Versus 9/11

Wikipedia: Friedman presents 11/9 (Berlin Wall falls, 1989) and 9/11 as symbols of two contending sorts of imagination. He argues that America must continue to be a "dream factory" exporting hope, rather than a fortress. To that end, he makes a plea to retire September 11, 2001, as a defining moment for the United States. Imagination, he asserts, is a product of narratives and social formation; the key to progress is the reinterpretation of narratives. He gives eBay as an example of the creation of a self-governing community, and cites the (relative) good fortune of Muslims in India. Oil resources are a factor in preventing representative institutions from developing, he argues. He visits a school for untouchables in India. In closing, Thomas Friedman asserts that the greatest dangers facing U.S. are "an excess of protectionism ... and excessive fears of competing".

Friedman's main message in closing his book is, "The flattening of the world, as I have tried to demonstrate in this book, has presented us with new opportunities, new challenges, new partners but also, alas, new dangers, particularly as Americans. It is imperative that we find the right balance among all of these. It is imperative that we be the best global citizens that we can be—because in a flat world, if you don't visit a bad neighborhood, it might visit you. And it is imperative that while we remain vigilant to the new threats, we do not let them paralyze us.

"To put it another way, the two greatest dangers we Americans face are an excess of protectionism—excessive fears of another 9/11 that prompt us to wall ourselves in, in search of personal security-and excessive fears of competing in a world of 11/9 that prompt us to wall ourselves off, in search of economic security. Both would be a disaster for us and for the world. Yes, economic competition in the flat world will be more equal and more intense. We Americans will have to work harder, run faster, and become smarter to make sure we get our share. But let us not underestimate our strengths or the innovation that could explode from the flat world when we really do connect all of the knowledge centers together. On such a flat earth, the most important attribute you can have is creative imagination— the ability to be the first on your block to figure out how all these enabling tools can be put together in new and exciting ways to create products, communities, opportunities, and profits. That has always been America's strength, because America was, and for now still is, the world's greatest dream machine.

"I cannot tell any other society or culture what to say to its own children, but I can tell you what I say to my own: The world is being flattened. I didn't start it and you can't stop it, except at a great cost to human development and your own future. But we can manage it, for better or for worse. If it is to be for better, not for worse, then you and your generation must not live in fear of either the terrorists or of tomorrow, of either al-Qaeda or of Infosys. You can flourish in this flat world, but it does take the right imagination and the right motivation. While your lives have been powerfully shaped by 9/11, the world needs you to be forever the generation of 11/9—the generation of strategic optimists, the generation with more dreams than memories, the generation that wakes up each morning and not only imagines that things can be better but also acts on that imagination every day."

While these lessons display concern for his children, he leaves it up to their imagination as to the way forward. Of course, his daughter attends Yale, and there Friedman found more insights for planning our futures while munching pizza, "In October 2005, my wife and I went up to New Haven to attend parents' weekend at Yale. We went out for a pizza lunch with our daughter and her roommates, and one roommate's boyfriend. I sat across from the boyfriend, Eric Stern, who was getting a PhD from Yale in biomedical engineering, with an expertise in nanotechnology. Eric is precisely the sort of young person we want the America education system to keep churning out."

Eric's father is a medical doctor and a science professor at Columbia. If only every kid in America had Eric's background and advantages and could graduate from Yale, all would be well in the Kingdom of Flat. All they need is a wealthy daddy, a degree from U.S.-President-producing Yale, and we are off to the races. But for those of us whose children do not breathe rarified air, Freidman tells them to use their imagination.

Let's revisit Friedman's fellow *New York Times* columnist who we quoted earlier. Paul Krugman paints a telling picture as he discusses the book, *Polarized America,* in his column, "Class War Politics." Krugman writes, "What the book shows, using a sophisticated analysis of Congressional votes and other data, is that for the past century, political polarization and economic inequality have moved hand in hand. Politics during the Gilded Age, an era of huge income gaps, was a nasty business—as nasty as it is today. The era of bipartisanship, which lasted for roughly a generation after World War II, corresponded to the high tide of America's middle class. That high tide began receding in the late 1970s, as middle-class incomes grew slowly at best while incomes at the top soared; and as income gaps widened, a deep partisan divide re-emerged.

"But if the real source of today's bitter partisanship is a Republican move to the right on economic issues, why have the last three elections been dominated by talk of terrorism, with a bit of religion on the side? Because a party whose economic policies favor a narrow elite needs to focus the public's attention elsewhere. And there's no better way to do that than accusing the other party of being unpatriotic and godless.

"Thus in 2004, President Bush basically ran as America's defender against gay married terrorists. He waited until after the election to reveal that what he really wanted to do was privatize Social Security."

Polarized America, looks at another contributor to polarization—immigration, "Immigration, meanwhile, has facilitated the move to the right: non-citizens, a larger share of the population and disproportionately poor, cannot vote; thus there is less political pressure from the bottom for redistribution than there is from the top against it. In 'the choreography of American politics' inequality feeds directly into political polarization, and polarization in turn creates policies that further increase inequality."

"Meanwhile, another *New York Times* columnist, Bob Herbert, describes in 'Laid Off and Left Out,' why we don't hear much anymore from what's left of the middle class. 'You don't hear much from the American worker anymore. Like battered soldiers at the end of a lost war, ordinary workers seem resigned to their diminished status.'

"The grim terms imposed on them include wage stagnation, the widespread confiscation of benefits (including pensions they once believed were guaranteed), and a permanent state of employment insecurity.'

"For an unnecessarily large number of Americans, the workplace has become a hub of anxiety and fear, an essential but capricious environment in which you might be shown the door at any moment.'

"In his book, *The Disposable American: Layoffs and Their Consequences,* Louis Uchitelle tells us that since 1984, when the U.S. Bureau of Labor Statistics started monitoring 'worker displacement,' at least 30 million full-time workers have been 'permanently separated from their jobs and their paychecks against their wishes.'"

Jim, an Amazon.com reviewer writes of Uchitelle's book, "Many view the relatively harmonious thirty years after WWII as an aberration in the generally contentious relations between employers and employees that has existed since the rise of industrialization. Yet layoffs in the context of globalization are new. Given the current political climate, it really seems quite likely that the situation will become far worse, literally transforming America into a Third World country of have and have-nots."

So, why don't these have-nots just go to Yale, get retrained for flat-world jobs and get on with their lives? Maybe they can even share a pizza and collaborate horizontally with Friedman.

Friedman's recommendations "to dream," and to use your "imaginations" in his concluding chapter is just fine for the Yale elite. But for the rest of us, it takes little imagination to know that the forces Friedman describes in his book are flattening what's left of America's middle class, which is the foundation for our democracy.

Here is how Bob Herbert describes the current state of affairs, "The gap between the rich and everybody else in this country is fast becoming an unbridgeable chasm. David Cay Johnston, in the latest installment of the *New York Times* series 'Class Matters,' wrote, 'It's no secret that the gap between the rich and the poor has been growing, but the extent to which the richest are leaving everybody else behind is not widely known.'

"Consider, for example, two separate eras in the lifetime of the baby-boom generation. For every additional dollar earned by the bottom 90 percent of the population between 1950 and 1970, those in the top 0.01 percent earned an additional $162. That gap has since skyrocketed. For every additional dollar earned by the bottom 90 percent between 1990 and 2002, Mr. Johnston wrote, each taxpayer in that top bracket brought in an extra $18,000.

"It's like chasing a speedboat with a rowboat.

"Put the myth of the American Dream aside. The bottom line is that it's becoming increasingly difficult for working Americans to move up in class. The rich are freezing nearly everybody else in place, and sprinting off with the nation's bounty.

"Many in the middle class are mortgaged to the hilt, maxed out on credit cards and fearful to the point of trembling that all they've worked for might vanish in a downsized minute."

Imagine that, Mr. Friedman.

No Issue Left Behind

As we discussed in the opening of this book, we can evaluate *The World is Flat* on what it ignores, as much as what it covers. In most of his presentation, Friedman solely looks at the labor market but ignores the issues of consumerism, national and household debt, raw

materials and other resource constraints, energy, and fixed investment markets. We assert that what he ignores is dangerous, for it
misinforms Presidents, industry captains and others that his book
influences.

Although there are others, we highlight nine aspects of globalization that were given little, if any, attention in Friedman's book. We
hope that by exploring these issues, you will want to begin a journey
to becoming a fully informed citizen on these and other aspects of
globalization that affect not only our economic lives, but also our
democracy. To restate what is at stake: Globalization is the most profound reorganization of the world since the Industrial Revolution.
Thus we must all become more informed about globalization if we
are to have a meaningful stake in determining our future.

1. Drivers of Twenty-first Century *Corporate* Globalization

While Friedman defines ten arbitrary flatteners, we consider that
the acceleration of twenty-first century corporate globalization is
being driven by:

1. *Containerized Cargo Shipping*—since 1956, "The Box," the stan-
    dardized shipping container, radically reduced the cost of ship-
    ping and removed or reduced distance as a barrier to trade;
2. *Continuing Advances in Global Communications*—began with the
    1957 launch of the Sputnik satellite, and now include fiber-optic
    and coax cables, faxes, cell phones, TV and the Internet; and
3. *Cheap Labor*—since the 1979 opening of China to Capitalism,
    followed by India and the Former Soviet Union, made cheap la-
    bor available worldwide;
4. *International Trade Organizations' Policies*—these policies, especially
    those of the World Trade Organization (1995), IMF, and World
    Bank, to date, mainly serve the interests of corporations and
    their lobbies, not the nations' citizens;
5. *The Deregulated Transnational Corporation*—with growing geopoliti-
    cal power ever since Reagan presidency, with its Reaganomics
    and trickle-down (Voodoo) economics, and now the grip of the
    corporate influence on the 2000–2008 White House and Con-
    gress. It is hard to call it trade when transnational corporations
    own their operations in multiple countries. For example, are we
    trading with Wal-Mart when we get our goods from their Chi-

nese operations? Do we get tax dollars from U.S. car makers when they make and sell their cars in China and no part of the business touches the U.S.? The AFL-CIO's Thea Lee writes, "Our corporate tax system is insanely inefficient and unfair. American taxpayers currently subsidize the offshoring of their own jobs (at a rate of at least $7 billion a year) through policies that exempt income earned offshore from corporate taxes. Very few other countries have similar systems, and most have some form of 'border adjustable' tax that exempts exports from sales or value-added taxes. Our current system taxes exports, while subsidizing the offshoring of jobs. We need a complete overhaul of our corporate tax system to address this self-inflicted wound."

The last two drivers are tightly interlinked. An informed citizenry is the foundation of a democracy. America's middle class is hurting but confused as to why, so it's important to understand what's really driving change in the economy. Globalization affects every Main Street and every dark alley in America.

Continually exclaiming about workflow software, uploading, outsourcing, offshoring, supply-chaining, insourcing, in-forming and steroids only befuddles, stupefies, baffles, dumbfounds, muddles, puzzles, misinforms, disorients, distracts and obfuscates the real issues facing ordinary Americans.

Economist Joseph Stiglitz, whom we have often quoted, writes, "Trade liberalization will also affect inequality. Opening up to trade does not make everyone in a country better off. Instead it changes the distribution of income and creates winners and losers. The standard economic argument is that the net gains from trade liberalization are positive so the gainers can compensate the losers and leave the country better off overall. Unfortunately, such compensation seldom occurs." These concerns are particularly relevant in America, where there is a general weakening of unemployment and medical insurance and other social safety nets.

In "A New Domestic and Global Strategy," Thea Lee writes, "The challenge we face today in the United States is how to engage in the global economy without decimating our own middle class and gutting our social regulatory system. The logic of global capitalism as currently practiced is to drive down workers' wages, weaken their bargaining power and strip away their social protections in both rich and poor countries, while simultaneously encouraging and celebrating the excesses of debt-driven consumerism."

Just consider the retired 70-something-year-old worker who just had her company dump its pension plan, give the plan over to the government, which will cut her monthly payout, and put the retiree on the burger-flipping lines. But elder workers won't be alone, as she will be working alongside millions of former middle class workers whose jobs were outsourced. Perhaps "globalization" should be taught in every high school civics class in America—and Stiglitz, not Friedman, should author the textbook.

2. Fair Trade or Free Trade?

Friedman totally ignores economist Joseph Stiglitz in his flat book. Stiglitz notes that the global trading framework of the past 50 years has been largely controlled by rich countries protecting their own interests. The ideology behind that framework is "Washington Consensus" neoliberalism, which holds that for all countries, at all times, the way to achieve economic growth, and thus the betterment of the human condition, is to remove, and to keep on removing, barriers to trade.

Unfortunately, as Stiglitz dryly points out, "It is difficult to identify the evidentiary source of the bullishness for unqualified trade liberalization." As Paul Kingsnorth writes in *The Independent*, "This is an economist's way of saying that the emperor has no clothes; that trade liberalisation has become a dogma that does not deliver. Indeed, poor countries which have grown rich have done so by doing the opposite of what the neoliberals told them to. 'To date,' Stiglitz writes, 'not one successful developing country has pursued a purely free market approach to development.' Forcing poor countries to open their markets, in fact, often simply entrenches poverty and inequality. What is needed, says Stiglitz, is a trading system which focuses on poverty-reduction and fairness."[26]

Stiglitz and co-author of *Free Trade for All*, Andrew Charlton, point out, "In 1994, Mexico entered the North American Free Trade Agreement (NAFTA), a far-reaching trade liberalization agreement with its northern neighbors, the United States and Canada. If ever there were an opportunity to demonstrate the value of free trade for a developing country, this was it. NAFTA gave Mexico access to the largest economy in the world, which was right next door.

"Ten years later, growth was slower than it had been in earlier decades (prior to 1980), mean real wages at the end of the decade were lower, and some of the poorest Mexicans had grown poorer as *subsidized* American farm products flooded the market and lowered the price received for their domestic production. Inequality and poverty both increased under NAFTA.

"[As we cited earlier in this book] NAFTA was not really a free trade agreement. America retained its agriculture subsidies. NAFTA pitted the heavily subsidized U.S. agribusiness sector against peasant producers and family farms in Mexico. U.S. farmers export many of their products into Mexico at costs far below those of the local market, driving down prices for local farmers. America also continued to use what were effectively non-tariff barriers to keep out some of Mexico's products.

"… these policies hurt rural livelihoods. One-fifth of Mexico's workers are employed in the agricultural sector, and 75 percent of Mexico's poverty is found in rural areas. While some large Mexican agribusiness sectors have expanded their exports, much of Mexico's rural sector is in crisis. Local farms are threatened by cheap imports from the United States, falling commodity prices and reduced government support. Four-fifths of the population of rural Mexico lives in poverty, and more than half are in extreme poverty. Many Mexicans are now in the swelling ranks of those illegally immigrating into the U.S."27

In the article, "Beyond NAFTA," Stiglitz and Charlton provide an example of how the tide of illegal immigration into the U.S. from Mexico could be reversed by making infrastructure investments in Mexico. "Along with such an infrastructure program, the three NAFTA countries could embark on a regional retirement program— a series of measures aimed at facilitating and promoting the voluntary relocation of retired US and Canadian citizens to Mexico. In the next thirty years, more than 100 million Americans will turn 65. Many will have a hard time affording a comfortable US retirement. One cheap and relatively easy part of the solution would be to let retirees follow the sun over the border by extending their Medicare coverage to Mexico, where the cost of living is much lower.

"By reimbursing Medicare-eligible patient expenses—perhaps at a discount to high US rates—at inspected and approved healthcare facilities in Mexico, and by negotiating with the Mexican government to insure adequate legal protection for retirees and their property, the United States could open the doors for, ultimately, millions of aging Baby Boomers to enjoy affordable and comfortable retirements south of the border. The effects on Mexico would be transforming: If 10 percent of the new retirees were to go to Mexico, the annual economic boost of their spending and Medicare payments alone would be roughly equal to 50 percent of Mexico's current GDP. Mexico would also gain from an increased demand for both skilled and unskilled healthcare workers."[28]

This makes sense, but will just, fair trade happen in the current framework of "unfair" free trade? Just try spending your Medicare benefits outside the U.S. It won't happen, even though the cost-benefit is enormous for the government, the insurance industry, and you.

Stop press! This just in from NBC: "June 14, 2006, Coral Gables, Fla.—In recent months, nearly 900 South Floridians have ordered prescription drugs from Canada, but they haven't gotten them because U.S. Customs seized the medications. Jacqueline Flick of Coral Gables gets her cholesterol-fighting drug Lipitor from Canada. In April, the U.S. government seized Flick's 90-day supply. 'I was stunned and my thought was that they were just trying to strong arm us into signing up for the government [Medicare] plan,' Flick said. U.S. Customs said the crackdown started in mid-November. They, of course, claim that there is no connection between the prescription-drug benefit and the seizure of senior citizens' prescription drugs. 'It's personal,' Flick said. 'It's my health. I don't feel the government should tell me what I have to spend for my medicine and from whom I buy it.' For a 90-day supply of 40 milligram pills, Flick pays a Canadian pharmacy $178. The price at CVS is almost $345."[29]

And we thought that Canada was part of NAFTA. You know, "free trade" and all that stuff.

Even *within* the borders of the United States, with the supposed wonderful Medicare prescription drug "benefit," remember that the government itself is not allowed, by law, to bargain using its bulk buying power with BigPharma companies.

These so-called free trade agreements don't just cause poverty outside the U.S., they also supersede American laws. The creation of the World Trade Organization (WTO) established an unelected group of bureaucrats who have claimed the power to regulate American global trade, a power that was once in the hands of the U.S. Congress. But it's not just the bureaucrats that are at play here; it's also the powerful corporate lobbies. Even free-trade economist, Jagdish Bhagwati, writes in his book, *In Defense of Globalization*, "We must consider the possibility that the multinationals have, through their interest-driven lobbying, helped set the rules in the world trading, intellectual property, aid, and other regimes that are occasionally harmful to the interests of the poor countries. A prime example of such harmful lobbying by corporations in recent years has involved intellectual property protection (IPP). The damage inflicted on the WTO system and on the poor nations has been substantial. In addition, pseudo-intellectual justification was adduced by pretending that IPP was a trade subject: [There is already an international organization—WIPO (World International Property Organization) to deal with Intellectual Property.] the magic words 'trade-related' were added to turn IPP into TRIPS (Trade-Related Intellectual Property Rights). Clearly the rules sought by the pharmaceutical companies are unnecessarily harmful to the poor countries. In particular, TRIPS should not be in the WTO at all."

3. Ricardo and National Industrial Policy

Friedman, who is neither a business writer nor an economist, passes judgment on the Ricardian theory of comparative advantage as he writes, "My mind just kept telling me, 'Ricardo is right, Ricardo is right, Ricardo is right." What does a real capitalist economist think?

Let's extend our discussion of "Chapter 5: America and Free Trade" and turn to Stephen Roach, chief economist at Morgan Stanley, "The global labor arbitrage adds a critical new and surprising wrinkle to globalization. The time-honored Ricardian models of comparative advantage have always broken down economies into two broad sectors—tradables (such as manufacturing) and nontradables (such as services).

"Good in theory.

"The theory was that rich high-wage economies would gladly give up market share in manufacturing to low-wage workers in poorer economies in exchange for lower-cost goods.

"This exchange would then prompt a migration of vulnerable workers in the rich countries from openly-tradable manufacturing to sheltered, non-tradable services industries.

"A tradable market?

"Economies in the developed world would then thrive as increasingly knowledge-based systems—and the developing world would flourish as a manufacturing center.

"My travels tell me that the theory isn't working as advertised. Globalization may well be win-win in the long run—but in the here and now, it is profoundly asymmetrical.

"Courtesy of the Internet, this model has now broken down. IT-enabled breakthroughs have not only revolutionized the logistics of supply-chain management in manufacturing. They have also transformed once non-tradable, information-based activities—such as software programming, engineering, design, accounting, lawyers, medical and financial analysis—into tradables.

"In an era increasingly dominated by the ultimate disruptive technology, the distinction between tradables and non-tradables has become blurred."[30]

Throughout the history of international trade, the nation has, and continues to have, a central role in creating comparative advantage. In contrast to Friedman's one-world, deregulated free-market, most Asian countries have used national policy to great advantage, while American national policy is no policy, leaving economic decision making to transnational corporations. Ricardo being theoretically right doesn't stop China from defining its specializations. To understand how America, as a nation, is at risk from a lack of national industrial policy, you can learn much from Clyde Prestowitz (see our discussion of "Chapter 5: America and Free Trade").

Continuing that discussion, let's turn to investigative reporter, Greg Palast's piece, "China Floats, America Sinks" where he provides a lesson in economics of globalization. "Don't take economics lessons from George Bush. Or Milton Friedman. Or Thomas Friedman. What that means, class, is don't believe the big, hot pile of hype that China's zooming economy is the result of that Red nation's adopting free market economic policies.

"If China is now a capitalist free-market state, then I'm Mariah Carey. China's economy has soared because it stubbornly refused the Free –and Friedman– Market mumbo-jumbo that government should stop controlling, owning and regulating industry.

"China's announcement that it would raise the cost of the Yuan covered over a more important notice that China would bar foreign control of its steel sector. China's leaders have built a powerhouse steel industry larger than ours by directing the funding, output, location and ownership of all factories. And rather than 'freeing' the industry through opening their borders to foreign competition, the Chinese, for steel and every other product, have shut their borders tight to foreigners except as it suits China's own needs.

"China won't join NAFTA or CAFTA or any of those free-trade clubs. In China, Chinese industry comes first. And it's still, Messrs.

Friedman, the *Peoples'* republic. Those Wal-Mart fashion designs called, chillingly, 'New Order,' are made in factories owned by the PLA, the Chinese Peoples' Liberation Army.

"In an interview just before he won the Nobel Prize in economics, Joe Stiglitz explained to me that China's huge financial surge—a stunning 9.5% jump in GDP this year [2005]—began with the government's funding and nurturing rural cooperatives, fledgling industry protected behind high, high trade barriers.

"It is true that China's growth got a boost from ending the blood-soaked self-flagellating madness of Mao's Cultural Revolution. And China, when it chooses, makes use of markets and market pricing to distribute resources. However, Chinese markets are as free as my kids: they can do whatever they want unless I say they can't.

"Yes, China is adopting elements of 'capitalism.' And that's the ugly part: real estate speculation in Shanghai making millionaires of Communist party boss relatives and bank shenanigans worthy of a Neil Bush.

"It is not the Guangdong skyscrapers and speculative bubble which allows China to sell us $162 billion more goods a year than we sell them. It is that China's government, by rejecting free-market fundamentalism, can easily conquer American markets where protection is now deemed passé.

"And that is why the Yuan has kicked the dollar's butt.

"America's only response is to have Alan Greenspan push up real interest rates so we can buy back our own dollars the Chinese won in the export game. The domestic result: U.S. wages drifting down to Mexican *maquiladora* levels.

"Am I praising China? Forget about it. This is one evil dictatorship which jails union organizers and beats, shackles and tortures those who don't kowtow to the wishes of Chairman Rob—Wal-Mart chief Robson Walton. (Funny how Mr. Bush never mentions the D-word, Democracy, to our Chinese suppliers.)

"Class dismissed."[31]

Interestingly, Chinese President Hu Jintau's formal dinner during his April 2006 four-day tour of America was not in Washington D.C., but was in Washington State at the home of Bill Gates. Why was the world's leader of the Communist Party the guest of the world's richest capitalist?

Could they have been discussing the idea of Bill Gates becoming the next U.N. secretary-general? As it becomes harder and harder to distinguish corporate decision-making from government policy-

making, it could happen, according to the analysis of management
guru, Kenichi Ohmae, as described in his book, *The Invisible Continent*.
Amazingly, there are some who still believe that George W. Bush is
in charge of the world.

Ohmae's invisible continent is a moving, unbounded world, con-
sisting of four dimensions: There's what you can see (old economy
commerce, like bricks-and-mortar retail); a borderless world in which
capital moves around, chasing the best products and the highest investment returns regardless of national origin; the cyber-world,
which has changed not only the way we do business but the way we
interact on a personal level; and the high multiples awarded to new
economy stocks, which are the basis of not only present wealth but
what anyone with a retirement plan hopes will be future comfort.

Meanwhile, many in that teen-aged country, America, are just beginning to think about what will have happened as early as 2010.
Some forecasts show that with an average growth rate of 8-10%,
China will, by 2010, have surpassed Japan, and by 2030, it will have
the world's largest economy. China's GDP could be double that of
the U.S. by 2050. Meanwhile, back in Washington, industrial policy is
left up to the "free market"—or, as we've already said, there is no
policy.

4. Debt and The Financialization of America

Globalization has an underbelly that Friedman chiefly ignores.
Globalization isn't just about what serf-like wages in China and India
are doing to America, it's also about what American transnational
corporations and neoliberals are doing to Americans, or more precisely what deregulated media and financial services companies are
encouraging Americans to do. That is consume, consume, consume
—no matter what—and do it on credit.

It's called "financialization," a state where financial services becomes the dominate component of a nation's gross domestic product (GDP). Economics commentator, Kevin Phillips defines financialization as a process whereby financial services, broadly construed,
take over the dominant economic, cultural, and political role in the
national economy. Phillips writes, "Part of what propelled financial
services were the profits gained from providing American households with artificial purchasing power—the loans that many took out
to splurge on consumption or to restore income levels they could no

longer attain from shrinking manufacturing or back-office wages."[32]
Here's what it looks like in the U.S.

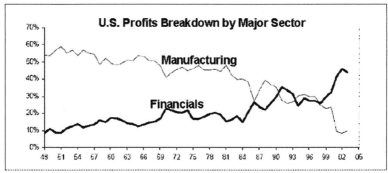

Source: Bridgewater Associates

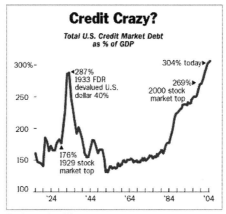

Source: Clapboard Hill Investment Partners; Barron's Magazine

In 2004, total credit market debt reached 304% of America's gross domestic product. In 1980, Americans collectively saved 7.4% of national income, by 1990, it had fallen to 4.5%, and in 2005, the savings rate went negative!

In "Debt and Denial," *New York Times* columnist and economist, Paul Krugman, wrote, "Last year America spent 57 percent more than it earned on world markets. That is, our imports were 57 percent larger than our exports.

"How did we manage to live so far beyond our means? By running up debts to Japan, China and Middle Eastern oil producers. We're as addicted to imported money as we are to imported oil. But this time our overseas borrowing isn't financing an investment boom: adjusted for the size of the economy, business investment is actually low by historical standards. Instead, we're using borrowed money to build houses, buy consumer goods and, of course, finance the federal budget deficit.

"In 2005 spending on home construction as a percentage of G.D.P. reached its highest level in more than 50 years. People who already own houses are treating them like A.T.M.s, converting home equity into spending money: last year the personal savings rate fell below zero for the first time since 1933. And it's a sign of our degraded fiscal state that the Bush administration actually boasted about a 2005 budget deficit of more than $300 billion, because it was a bit lower than the 2004 deficit.

"It all sounds unsustainable. And it is."

Consider the remarks of Paul Volcker, Former U.S. Federal Reserve Bank Chairman, on April 10, 2005, "Under the placid surface [of the economy], there are disturbing trends: huge imbalances, disequilibria, risks—call them what you will. Altogether the circumstances seem to me as dangerous and intractable as any I can remember, and I can remember quite a lot."[33]

Deregulation of the financial services industry is one part of the growing neoliberal power structure in the United States, and the growing financialization of the country. And it starts at an early age in one's life. In "Don't Leave College Without It," Taylor Loyal wrote, "Jon Selden never had a credit card before he went to college. But a few weeks after arriving at Brigham Young University, he received an offer mailed to his dorm room for a preapproved Citibank card. Before Selden even managed to find a job or establish a credit history, he was running up thousands of dollars in debt.

"Credit card companies like Citibank aren't the only institutions profiting from student spending. Like other colleges and universities across the country, Brigham Young has done a lucrative business with big lenders, enhancing university revenues at the expense of students. BYU received an estimated $70,000 last year in exchange for stuffing offers for Citibank cards into 1 million shopping bags at the university bookstore. The University of Tennessee has a seven-year, $16.5 million deal with First USA that gives the company the names and addresses of alumni, employees, and more than 40,000 students. The University of Michigan and Michigan State have struck similar deals with MBNA, the self-proclaimed 'world's largest independent credit card issuer,' worth an estimated $14 million.

"By the time Jon Selden graduated from Brigham Young last year, he had accumulated $8,000 in debt. Now enrolled in law school, he lives with his parents and waits tables rather than filing for bankruptcy. 'Was I stupid to run up that debt?' says Selden. 'You bet. But I was 18.' Selden may have been stupid, but others ended up less than stupid.

"Every major university also has students burdened by massive debts that they have little hope of paying off. Sean Moyer, a National Merit Scholar, racked up more than $12,000 on 12 credit cards while enrolled at the universities of Oklahoma and Texas. In 1998, even though he was working two jobs to pay off the cards, he believed his debt would prevent him from attending law school. 'He just said he felt like he was a failure,' recalls his mother, Janne O'Donnell. Nine days after confessing his fears, the 22–year-old Moyer hung himself in his bedroom closet." [34]

In "A New Domestic and Global Strategy," Thea Lee writes, "The United States is running a current account deficit of more than $700 billion a year to fund consumption we can't afford. This is not financially sustainable. Meanwhile, many workers in developing countries work twelve to sixteen hours a day, in dangerous conditions, without the right to form an independent union, at poverty pay, so that transnational corporations can boost their bottom line. That is not politically sustainable.

"That the national debt is currently over $8 trillion is only the tip of the iceberg. There has also been an explosion of corporate debt, state and local bonded debt, international debt through huge trade imbalances, and consumer debt (mostly in the form of credit-card balances and aggressively marketed home-mortgage packages). Taken together, this present and future debt may exceed $70 trillion." [35]

In his blog,[36] Barry Ritholtz, Chief Market Strategist for Ritholtz Research, wrote, "The remorseless decline in wages as a percentage of personal income has reached an historic low of 62%. Meanwhile, consumer spending as a percentage of wages continues to spiral upward. In the past three years, Stephanie Pomboy of MacroMavens reckons, shop-happy consumers, cheerfully determined to live beyond their means, leaned a lot more heavily on borrowings ($675 billion of non-mortgage debt) than paychecks ($530 billion) to cover the $1.3 trillion increase in their spending. This may be great while it lasts, but it cannot go on forever. Trigger points for stopping America's consumption spree include higher interest rates, record-high gasoline prices and the rising cost of just about everything. And then, or course, when foreign lenders decide they are holding too many dollars, all hell could break loose as 'free money' disappears." [37]

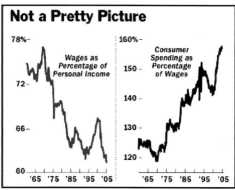

Source: Stephanie Pomboy, MacroMavens,
Baron's, April 25, 2005.

In *The Indebted Society*, economists James Medoff and Andrew Harless advance the argument that as debt burgeoned in the 1980s, it also realigned political power. When debt becomes more important in society, lenders become more important, making them more powerful. They then tend to influence policy, and today's deregulated financial services companies are free to entice debtors with low interest rate consolidation packages, and then jack up interest rates to *usury* levels after the first late payment. By 2005, household debt reached such high levels that it triggered the enactment of tough new federal bankruptcy laws—to protect lenders, not debtors. We now have what economists Noriel Roubini and Brad Setser have coined as "the borrower-industrial complex," led by credit-card companies and other lenders that have grown up around ever-more desperate borrowers and their ever-growing needs.

In April, 2004, Brett Arends of *The Boston Herald* attended a private presentation to a select group of fund managers, by Stephen Roach, the chief economist at Morgan Stanley. In his report on the presentation, Arends wrote that Roach predicted, "America has no better than a 10 percent chance of avoiding economic Armageddon."

"To finance its current account deficit with the rest of the world, he said, America has to import $2.6 billion in cash. Every working day.

"That is an amazing 80 percent of the entire world's net savings.

"Sustainable? Hardly.

"Meanwhile, he notes that household debt is at record levels. Twenty years ago the total debt of U.S. households was equal to half the size of the economy. Today the figure is 85 percent.

"Nearly half of new mortgage borrowing is at flexible interest rates, leaving borrowers much more vulnerable to rate hikes. Americans are already spending a record share of disposable income paying their interest bills. And interest rates haven't even risen much yet."[38]

Although Friedman largely ignores the debt "externality," debt and the financialization of America are indeed menacing aspects of his flat world. And if Roach is right, these issues cannot be ignored much longer.

5. America's Former Middle Class

Congressman Bernie Sanders, the only Independent in the House of Representatives, reflects a growing concern about globalization and America's working families, "The decline of the American middle class is not just one of the issues out there. It is *the* issue in the United States today. In terms of its impact on middle income and working families, there can be no debate that our unfettered free trade policy is an unqualified disaster. Millions of jobs have been lost. Wages are being pushed lower. Fringe benefits are being scaled back significantly. American workers are being forced to compete with desperate workers living in countries with very little political or economic rights who are paid as little as $0.20 an hour. Free trade with the U.S. also lowers the standard of living for workers abroad as well, as demonstrated by the Mexican experience under NAFTA. The big Money interests are delighted. Working Americans are deserted—and they know it."[39]

In "The Middle Class on the Precipice," in *Harvard Magazine*,[40] Harvard's Elizabeth Warren writes, "Why are so many moms in the workforce? Surely, some are lured by a great job, but millions more need a paycheck, plain and simple. In just one generation, millions of mothers have gone to work, transforming basic family economics. The typical middle-class household in the United States is no longer a one-earner family, with one parent in the workforce and one at home full-time. Instead, the majority of families with small children now have both parents rising at dawn to commute to jobs so they can both pull in paychecks.

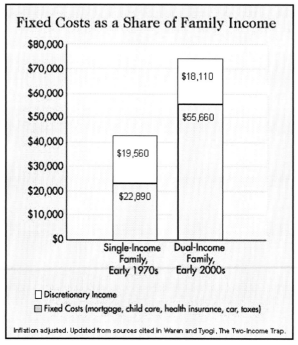

Fixed Costs as a Share of Family Income

"Today's family has no margin for error. There is no leeway to cut back if one earner's hours are cut or if the other gets sick. There is no room in the budget if someone needs to take off work to care for a sick child or an elderly parent. The modern American family is walking a high wire without a net. Income risk has shifted in other ways as well. Incomes are less dependable today. Layoffs, outsourcing, and other workplace changes have trebled the odds of a significant interruption in a single generation. The shift from one income to two doubled the risks again, as both Mom and Dad face the possibility of unemployment. Their basic situation is far riskier than that of their parents a generation earlier. If anything—anything at all—goes wrong, then today's two-income family is in big trouble."

In "The Collapse of the Middle Class," Rep. Sanders summarizes that flattening, "The corporate media doesn't talk about it much, but the United States is rapidly on its way to becoming three separate nations.

"First, there are a small number of incredibly wealthy people who own and control more and more of our country. Second, there is a shrinking middle class in which ordinary people are, in most instances, working longer hours for lower wages and benefits. Third, an increasing number of Americans are living in abject poverty—going hungry and sleeping out on the streets.

"There has always been a wealthy elite in this country, and there has always been a gap between the rich and the poor. But the disparities in wealth and income that currently exist in this country have not been seen in over a hundred years. Today, the richest 1 percent own more wealth than the bottom 95 percent, and the CEOs of large corporations earn more than 500 times what their average employees make. The nation's 13,000 wealthiest families, 1/100th of one percent of the population, receive almost as much income as the poorest 20 million families in America.

"While the rich get richer and receive huge tax breaks from the White House, the middle class is struggling to keep its head above water. The unemployment rate rose to a nine-year high of 6.4 percent in June 2003. There are now 9.4 million unemployed, up more than 3 million since just before Bush became President. Since March 2001, we have lost over 2.7 million jobs in the private sector, including two million decent-paying manufacturing jobs—ten percent of our manufacturing sector. Frighteningly, the hemorrhaging of decent paying jobs is now moving into the white-collar sector. Forrester Research Inc. predicts that at least 3.3 million information technology jobs will be lost to low-wage countries by 2015 with the expansion of digitization, the Internet and high-speed data networks.

"But understanding the pain and anxiety of the middle class requires going beyond the unemployment numbers. There are tens of millions of fully employed Americans who today earn, in inflation adjusted-dollars, less money than they received 30 years ago. In 1973, private-sector workers in the United States were paid on average $9.08 an hour. Today, in real wages, they are paid $8.33 per hour—more than 8 percent lower. Manufacturing jobs that once paid a living wage are now being done in China, Mexico and other low-wage countries as corporate America ships its plants abroad.

"With Wal-Mart replacing General Motors as our largest employer, many workers in the service economy not only earn low wages but also receive minimal benefits. Further, as the cost of health insurance and prescription drugs soar, more and more employers are forcing workers to assume a greater percentage of their health care costs. It is not uncommon now that increases in health care costs surpass the wage increases that workers receive—leaving them even further behind. With the support of the Bush Administration many companies are also reducing the pensions they promised to their older workers—threatening the retirement security of millions of Americans.

"One of the manifestations of the collapse of the middle class is the increased number of hours that Americans are now forced to work in order to pay the bills. Today, the average American employee works, by far, the longest hours of any worker in the industrialized world. And the situation is getting worse. According to statistics from the International Labor Organization the average American last year worked 1,978 hours, up from 1,942 hours in 1990—an increase of almost a week of work. We are now putting more hours into our work than at any time since the 1920s. Sixty-five years after the formal establishment of the 40-hour work week under the Fair Labor Standards Act, almost 40 percent of Americans now work more than 50 hours a week.

"And if the middle class is having it tough, what about the 33 million people in our society who are living in poverty, up 1.3 million in the past two years? What about the 11 million trying to make it on a pathetic minimum wage of $5.15 an hour? What about the 42 million who lack any health insurance? What about the 3.5 million people who will experience homelessness in this year, 1.3 million of them children? What about the elderly who can't afford the outrageously high cost of the prescription drugs they need? What about the veterans who are on VA waiting lists for their health care?

"This country needs to radically rethink our national priorities. The middle class is the backbone of America and it cannot be allowed to disintegrate. We need to revitalize American democracy, and create a political climate where government makes decisions which reflect the needs of all the people, and not just wealthy campaign contributors. We need to see the middle class expand, not collapse."

Bye, bye, Miss American Pie, drove my Chevy to the levee but the levee was dry.

6. Privatization of the Commons

Agriculture, indigenous people's resources, water, genes, medicines—they are all increasingly being privatized and placed in the hands of transnational corporations. The field of economics has always addressed both private goods and public goods. But today's neoliberal philosophy views all as private goods.

Should some goods be off limits to corporate globalization and, if so, which ones?

To answer this question, we'll turn to the concept of the commons. But first, let us hear from Indian physicist, Vandana Shiva. Dr. Shiva is the Director of the Research Foundation for Science, Technology and Natural Resource Policy in New Delhi. She had been invited to have an interview with Friedman as part of a documentary he was producing. More on that in a minute, but first here is part of what she had to say about *The World is Flat* in a 2005 article, "The Polarized World Of Globalisation," "By presenting open sourcing in the same category as outsourcing and off shore production, Friedman hides corporate greed, corporate monopolies and corporate power, and presents corporate globalisation as human creativity and freedom. This is deliberate dishonesty, not just result of flat vision. That is why in his stories from India he does not talk about Dr. Hamid of CIPLA who provided AIDS medicine to Africa for $200 when U.S. corporations wanted to sell them for $20,000 and who has called W.T.O.'s patent laws 'genocidal.' And in spite of Friedman's research team having fixed an appointment with me to fly down to Bangalore to talk about farmers' suicides for the documentary Friedman refers to, Friedman cancelled the appointment at the last minute.

"You know in India, we believe in reincarnation. This life is just a passing thing. I have come for a day to the valley, this life is one step. In India, you could never despair because there was another life and another life and another and another and another and another. And so what if things go wrong in this one. But globalization has literally changed even that optimism of reaching incarnation in India, and farmers are committing suicide (20,000 farmers in 2003) 735 suicides in one state in the last month alone. And all of this has happened after the big companies came into the seed sector in India—started to sell costly seed and started to sell expensive chemicals linked to the seed and started to sell them with very aggressive advertising.

"People always say, 'But why do the farmers buy it?' Because Monsanto doesn't come selling seed as Monsanto. Monsanto comes firstly, selling seed through Indian companies they have bought up, but even more importantly, they hire all our gods and divinities. So in Punjab, they have Guru Nanak posters, who is the founder of the Sikh religion with Round Up and their seeds. "Well, Monsanto seeds are this life-saving miracle. And you can imagine peasants who have some association with the mythology if the advertising of the companies comes through that mythology, you are not suddenly going to have a mind switch in the peasantry and say stop believing in your mythology. You are going to still believe this is the Hanumanji bringing you the ultimate deliverance from poverty. And then they bring lovely videos, they show American farmers with big combines and rich tractors and say, you will be like that. The farmers get trapped within the season.

"Every year I do a public hearing, and the last public hearing I did was in February and we called, I think, about 200 families where people had committed suicide. In every family, it was the women who were left behind. Because you know, the men go into the town to play a game of cards, drink a bit of Indian liquor, have a smoke. And that's when they're trapped by the agents of the companies. Usually the family doesn't even know that this seed is ten times more costly, that this chemical is a poison. They have no idea, and eventually when the men can't pay back the debt, they drink the same poisons to end their lives.

"One myth that separates affluence from poverty, is the assumption that if you produce what you consume, you do not produce. This is the basis on which the production boundary is drawn for national accounting that measures economic growth. Such myths contribute to the mystification of growth and consumerism, but they also hide the real processes that create poverty. The market economy dominated by capital is not the only economy. Development has, however, been based on the growth of the market economy.

"The invisible costs of development have been the destruction of two other economies: nature's processes and people's survival. The ignorance or neglect of these two vital economies is the reason why development has posed a threat of ecological destruction and a threat to human survival, both of which, however, have remained 'hidden negative externalities' of the development process. Instead of being seen as results of exclusion, they are presented as 'those left behind.' Instead of being viewed as those who suffer the worst burden of unjust growth in the form of poverty, they are falsely presented as those not touched by growth.

"Trade and exchange of goods and services have always existed in human societies, but these were subjected to nature's and people's economies. The elevation of the domain of the market and man-made capital to the position of the highest organizing principle for societies has led to the neglect and destruction of the other two organizing principles—ecology and survival—which maintain and sustain life in nature and society.

"Modern economies and concepts of development cover only a negligible part of the history of human interaction with nature. For centuries, principles of sustenance have given human societies the material basis of survival by deriving livelihoods directly from nature through self-provisioning mechanisms. Limits in nature have been respected and have guided the limits of human consumption. In most countries of the South large numbers of people continue to derive their sustenance in the survival economy which remains invisible to market-oriented development. All people in all societies depend on nature's economy for survival.

"When the organizing principle for society's relationship with nature is sustenance, nature exists as a *commons*. It becomes a *resource* when profits and accumulation become the organizing principles and create an imperative for the exploitation of resources for the market. Without clean water, fertile soils and crop and plant genetic diversity, human survival is not possible. These commons have been destroyed by economic development, resulting in the creation of a new contradiction between the economy of natural processes and the survival economy, because those people deprived of their traditional land and means of survival by development are forced to survive on an increasingly eroded nature.

"People do not die for lack of incomes. They die for lack of access to resources. The indigenous people in the Amazon, the mountain communities in the Himalaya, peasants whose land has not been appropriated and whose water and biodiversity has not been destroyed by debt creating industrial agriculture are ecologically rich, even though they do not earn a dollar a day.

"On the other hand, even at five dollars a day, people are poor if they have to buy their basic needs at high prices. Indian peasants who have been made poor and pushed into debt over the past decade to create markets for costly seeds and agrichemicals through economic globalisation are ending their lives in thousands. When seeds are patented and peasants will pay $1 trillion in royalties, they will be $1 trillion poorer. Patents on medicines increase costs of AIDS drugs from $200 to $20,000, and cancer drugs from $2,400 to $36,000 for a year's treatment. When water is privatized, and global corporations make $1 trillion from commodification of water, the poor are poorer by $1 trillion."

Returning to the commons, Canadian Richard Bocking wrote in "Reclaiming the Commons,"[41] "Once upon a time, nobody owned anything. Or perhaps, everybody owned everything. The world, and everything in it, was a gigantic 'commons.' 'The Commons' was the name used in medieval England to describe parcels of land that were used 'in common' by peasant farmers, very few of whom owned enough land to survive upon. Their lives depended upon access to and use of a shared landscape that provided many necessities: grazing land for their oxen or their livestock, water in streams, ponds or wells, wood and fuel from a forest. The land was probably owned by a titled notable, but the importance of the commons to the survival of the population was so obvious that strict rules, recognized by the courts, required landowners to ensure the commons remained available for use by peasant farmers. That access was considered a right, which people took for granted, much as we assume we have a right to breathe air. Property was thought of as a collection of rights as much as it was title to a piece of land; and often those rights took precedence.

"But landowners began to imagine how much richer they could be if they could remove 'the commoners,' and use the land themselves. They began to plant hedges or otherwise bar the way onto lands that had been used and depended upon by nearby families for centuries. This practice became known as 'enclosure.' Parliament bowed to the will of wealthy landowners and passed the Enclosure Acts, stripping commoners of their property rights. By 1895, about half of one percent of the population of England and Wales owned almost 99 percent of the land. Sheep grazed former common lands, while peasants starved, or were forced into the cities—which is why London was the first city to have a million inhabitants. Some provided labour for the industrial revolution, but tens of thousands of commoners were forced into vagrancy and destitution. In Scotland people were packed onto ships, often at gunpoint, and transported across the ocean to the Americas in conditions often as bad as those on slave ships.

"And so 'commons' and 'enclosure' have become words loaded with significance. The term 'commons,' derived from that ancient usage in the English countryside, is now applied to those things to which we have rights simply by being members of the human family. The air we breathe, the fresh water we drink, the seas, forests, and mountains, the genetic heritage through which all life is transmitted, the diversity of life itself. There is the commons that humankind has created—language, a wealth of scientific, cultural, and technical knowledge accumulated over the ages, our public universities, our health and education systems, the broadcast spectrum, our public utilities. There are the commons that we have specifically declared to be public assets, like our parks.

"A 'commons,' then, is synonymous with community, cooperation, and respect for the rights and preferences of others. 'Enclosure,' on the other hand, refers to exclusion, possession, monopoly, and personal or corporate gain. Just as 'enclosure' removed the rights to the commons of peasant farmers before the industrial revolution, Europeans carried the principle of enclosing the commons with them during the era of colonization, declaring any land without institutions or evidence of European-style sovereignty to be Terra Nullius, (vacant land) even though the population of the Americas, for example, is estimated to have exceeded 100 million before colonization. Except for tiny inadequate reserves, the land was 'enclosed;' that is, restricted for the use of the newcomers, and barred to those who had used it from time immemorial. The process continues today in such places as Indonesia, India, the Amazon, or Africa, where indigenous populations or small farmers see the land they have long occupied enclosed in favour of large scale ranching and farming operations, or for exploitation by mining, oil and logging corporations that frequently destroy the landscape and pollute air and water.

"Enclosure of the commons has been going on for centuries, but today it is being practised on a scale and at a speed unimaginable only a few years ago. Just a few examples of enclosure as it is being practised today: the determination of a few large corporations to privatize as much as possible of one of our most important commons, *fresh water*. The privatization of forests here and around the world through grants of tenure that exclude communities that did or could prosper through a commons regime; the enclosure of that miracle upon which life depends, the seed, once freely available for saving, sharing and replanting, now increasingly patented and controlled by a handful of giant chemical and biotechnology corporations.

"The genetic basis of life itself is being enclosed and corporatized through the development of intellectual property regimes that are being forced on the entire world under intellectual property terms of the World Trade Organization. This only became a practical possibility in 1980 when the United States first approved the patenting of living matter. Once patented, the genetics of a seed becomes an industrial secret and is unavailable, or available only at great cost, for others to improve upon. So the privatization of seed breeding tends to stifle agricultural science, and devastate entire farming systems.

"The enforcement of intellectual property rights enables Northern industrial nations to enclose or appropriate genetic resources and knowledge from the South. Over 99% of all patents on living organisms are held in the North. Biotechnology corporations roam the world searching for seeds with desirable characteristics. They modify perhaps a single gene, then patent and acquire exclusive rights over a plant that may have been developed over centuries by traditional farmers in a developing country. In this way, ownership and control of the world's seed diversity, most of it in the third world, is being transferred to transnational corporations based in the industrialized nations, principally the United States.

"Indigenous peoples and family farmers around the world are demanding an end to this process, often called 'biopiracy.' The patenting of life will, they claim, undermine their food security and lead to a disintegration of their communal values and practices. Local cooperatives are fighting transnational biotech corporations through movements like 'Seeds of Freedom' in India. As Vandana Shiva writes, 'monopoly ownership of life creates an unprecedented crisis for agricultural and food security, by transforming biological resources from commons into commodities.'

"Canola was developed by Canadian scientists for Canadian farmers over a period of 25 years in public research facilities paid for by all of us. Dr. Baldur Stefanson, a University of Manitoba scientist recognized as a 'father of canola,' explained with some bitterness that 75 percent of canola seed is now controlled by global corporations.

"Our public universities have become particularly vulnerable targets for enclosure by corporate interests. Science, and knowledge generally, has long been considered one of the great 'commons' of mankind. But corporate control in fields like genetic engineering is changing the way science is practiced, and threatening the basic function of our universities. In the normal practice of science, researchers publish their results so that colleagues around the world can verify or disprove their results, or use them as a springboard from which to press the work further. In biotech or similar research, the watchword is secrecy and the goal is speeding patented products to market. You don't publish without corporate permission, and you certainly don't publish anything that might reflect unfavourably on the product the company is pushing. One University of Victoria biochemist sadly described for me the loss of collegiality amongst his colleagues since corporate presence became palpable on the campus.

"When Jonas Salk was asked why he didn't patent his polio vaccine, he is reported to have said that it would make as much sense to patent sunlight - his vaccine belonged to everyone. Great scientists don't desist from doing research just because they don't have ties to a corporation that will make them rich if they keep their work secret.

"The infiltration of corporations into universities is in part due to reduced public funding for research and higher education. Since the corporate funding that universities seek and accept to make up this loss is largely devoted to the search for patentable products, other, often more important research, is neglected. The role of the university in society shifts, as University of Toronto philosopher James R. Brown described in an essay in the journal 'Science' that he called 'Privatizing the University - the New Tragedy of the Commons.' The corporate takeover of universities in the United States was documented not long ago in an Atlantic Monthly article entitled 'The Kept University.'

"A principal goal of institutions such as the World Trade Organization, the International Monetary Fund, the World Bank and the trade treaties they enforce is to ensure free corporate access to the commons of nations around the world, and to prevent communal values in those nations from being imposed on foreign corporations. And so a relatively small number of gigantic corporations, armed with WTO-endowed rights and relatively unencumbered with responsibility, roam the world looking for the richest resources and the most compliant governments, the least onerous environmental, health and safety regulations, and the lowest wages.

"The World Bank and the IMF promote and finance export agriculture, a huge enclosure project that drives small farmers off the land and into the cities while eliminating sustainable, self-sufficient food production systems. Enclosure is one of the principal reasons that 800 million people are hungry in a world that actually produces enough food for everyone.

"The newest development in globalization, the GATS or General Agreement on Trade in Services, is presently under negotiation by members of the WTO. It is aimed directly at some of our most treasured commons. Health-care, education, social services, and water resources—all would be open to exploitation and privatization by transnational corporations under terms of the GATS. It would appear that globalization is the new colonization, and trade treaties are its gunboats.

"Concern about the global commons and its enclosure is growing quickly. It encompasses most environmental issues, and the moral questions involved require the awareness of communities like ours.

Efforts throughout the world aimed at reclaiming the commons include the growing movement against corporate globalization, the many environmental movements, the alternative media movement, and efforts to prevent corporate takeover of water. Activists from more than 50 countries are promoting a treaty to establish the earth's gene pool as a global commons.

"Reclaiming the commons in its many forms, and accepting responsibility for its stewardship, in spirit and in fact, should be a defining issue of our time. The land we tread, the air we breathe, the water we drink, the biodiversity upon which life depends and the genetic code that expresses it, the knowledge and culture we inherited and enriched, can only be passed on unimpaired to future generations if they remain integral elements of 'the commons.'"

This section may seem overly long for this little book. But it sheds light on aspects of globalization that Friedman gives little, or no, treatment in his overly long book. Dr. Shiva elaborates, "Friedman presents a 0.1% picture and hides 99.9%. And in the 99.9% are Monsanto's seed monopolies and the suicides of thousands. In the eclipsed 99.9% are the 25 million women who disappeared in high growth areas of India because a commodified world has rendered women a dispensable sex. In the hidden 99.9% economy are thousands of tribal children in Orissa, Maharashtra, Rajasthan who died of hunger because the public distribution system for food has been dismantled to create markets for agribusiness. The world of the 99.9% has grown poorer because of the economic globalisation.

"The movements against economic globalisation and maldevelopment are movements to end poverty by ending the exclusions, injustices and ecological non-sustainability that are the root causes of poverty.

"The $50 billion of 'aid' North to South is a tenth of $500 billion flow South to North as interest payments and other unjust mechanisms in the global economy imposed by World Bank, IMF. With privatization of essential services and an unfair globalisation imposed through W.T.O, the poor are being made poorer. Indian peasants are losing $26 billion annually just in falling farm prices because of dumping and trade liberalization. As a result of unfair, unjust globalisation, which is leading to corporate, take over of food and water. More than $5 trillion will be transferred from poor people to rich countries just for food and water. The poor are financing the rich. If we are serious about ending poverty, we have to be serious about ending the unjust and violent systems for wealth creation which create poverty by robbing the poor of their resources, livelihoods and incomes."

How far should markets go? They generally deal well with private goods, but what about public goods like drinking water and clean air? The WTO has advocated the privatization of drinking water, clean air, and some life forms via TRIPS (Trade-Related Intellectual Property Rights) and genetic engineering. Are fresh water, clean air, and biodiversity part of a global commons? A fundamental human right? Or are they commodities, to be exchanged for capital? If they are privatized, what will be the fate of the billions of humans with no access to capital, who live near starvation, with less access to food and water than they did a decade ago? In essence, Joseph Stiglitz, like President Theodore Roosevelt, argues that people should govern markets; markets should not govern people.

7. Not Killing the Earth

In 1855, Chief Seattle wrote a letter to President Pierce about the Native American's relationship to the Earth and natural resources, "Will you teach your children what we have taught our children? That the Earth is our Mother? What befalls the Earth befalls all the sons of the Earth. This we know: The Earth does not belong to Man, Man belongs to the Earth. All things are connected like the blood which unites us all. Man did not weave the web of life, he is merely a strand in it. Whatever he does to the web, he does to himself.

"Even the white man, whose God walks and talks with him as friend to friend, cannot be exempt from the common destiny. We may be brothers after all. We shall see. One thing we know, which the white man may one day discover—our God is the same God. You may think now that you own Him as you wish to own our land: but you cannot. He is the God of man, and His compassion is equal for the red man and the white. This earth is precious to Him, and to harm the earth is to heap contempt upon its Creator.

"The Whites, too, shall pass; perhaps sooner than all other tribes. Contaminate your bed, and you will one night suffocate in your own waste."[42]

Hawken, Lovins and Lovins wrote in their book, *Natural Capitalism*, "For all the world to live as an American or Canadian, we would need two more earths to satisfy everyone, three more still if population should double, and twelve earths altogether if worldwide standards of living should double over the next forty years."

Hawken wrote in 1997, "The U.S. is far better at creating waste—1 million pounds per person per year—than products. Fresh Kills on Staten Island is the world's largest landfill, providing a repository for the garbage of New York City. Covering 4 square miles and more than 100 feet deep, it contains 2.9 billion cubic feet of trash, including 100 million tons of newspaper, paint cans, potato peels, cigarette butts, chicken bones, dryer lint, and an occasional corpse. New Yorkers dump 26 million pounds of trash at Fresh Kills daily. But as massive as Fresh Kills is, it takes in just 0.02 percent of the waste generated in the United States. Every day, Americans dispose of an additional 5,300 times as much waste elsewhere. Americans, who have the largest material requirements in the world, each directly or indirectly use an average of 125 pounds of material every day, or about 23 tons per year. Furthermore, domestic figures for material flows do not account for the waste generated overseas on our behalf. For example, the Freeport-McMoRan gold mine in Irian Jaya annually dumps 66 pounds of tailings and toxic waste into Indonesian rivers for every man, woman, and child in the United States. Only a tiny fraction of the 125,000 tons of daily waste material comes to the United States as gold. The rest remains there.

"Total wastes, excluding wastewater, exceed 50 trillion pounds a year in the United States. (A trillion is a big number. To count to 50 trillion at the rate of one numeral per second would require the cumulative and total lifetimes of 23,000 people.) If you add wastewater, the total flow of American waste equals at least 250 trillion pounds. Less than 5 percent of the total waste stream actually gets recycled—primarily paper, glass, plastic, aluminum, and steel."[43]

In "Making Poverty History and the History of Poverty," Dr. Vandana Shiva writes, "Garbage is the waste of a throwaway society—ecological societies have never had garbage. Homeless children are the consequences of impoverishment of communities and families who have lost their resources and livelihoods. These are images of the perversion and externalities of a non-sustainable, unjust, inequitable economic growth model. Trade and exchange of goods and services have always existed in human societies, but these were subjected to nature's and people's economies. The elevation of the domain of the market and man-made capital to the position of the highest organizing principle for societies has led to the neglect and destruction of the other two organizing principles—ecology and survival— which maintain and sustain life in nature and society.

"Modern economies and concepts of development cover only a negligible part of the history of human interaction with nature. When the organizing principle for society's relationship with nature is sustenance, nature exists as a commons. It becomes a resource when profits and accumulation become the organizing principles and create an imperative for the exploitation of resources for the market. Without clean water, fertile soils and crop and plant genetic diversity, human survival is not possible. These commons have been destroyed by economic development, resulting in the creation of a new contradiction between the economy of natural processes and the survival economy, because those people deprived of their traditional land and means of survival by development are forced to survive on an increasingly eroded nature." [44]

Natural Capitalism puts forward a new approach for protecting the biosphere and for improving profits and competitiveness. Some very simple changes to the way we run our businesses, built on advanced techniques for making resources more productive, can yield startling benefits both for today's share-holders and for future generations. It's what capitalism might become if its largest category of capital—the natural capital of ecosystem services—were properly valued. The journey to natural capitalism involves four major shifts in business practices, all vitally interlinked: dramatically increase the productivity of natural resources; shift to biologically inspired production models; move to a solutions-based business model; and reinvest in natural capital. Hawken, Lovins and Lovins provide a roadmap to natural capitalism, but there are also those on the planet that have already arrived at that destination; indigenous peoples who already live with nature, like Chief Seattle's people before the white man came to wrest away those resources.

8. Beyond Unipolarity: A Tripolar World

Friedman talks little about national boundaries other than nation-states being a source of friction to his flat world, "The biggest source of friction, of course, has always been the nation-state, with its clearly defined boundaries and laws." But it turns out that redrawing national boundaries could be a key globalization issue, for it won't likely be the transnational corporations flattening cultures and national identities. Though much has been written about geopolitical forces and how nations interact in the pursuit of power, in their book, *Tectonic Shift*, Professors Jagdish Sheth and Rajendra Sisodia offered a different view and concluded that there will likely be a geoeconomic realignment.

They note that over the past 200 years, the world's trade and investment streams have flowed east-west, mostly above the equator, e.g., North America, Western Europe and Japan, with very little crossover to the south. Thus, developed countries traded mostly with other developed nations, never attempting any degree of economic integration with underdeveloped countries to the south. But because the mature economies of the north are saddled with escalating social costs and aging populations, they will have the problem of sustaining the growth that made them preeminent in the global economy. For that reason, Sheth and Sisodia observe that the world is now becoming realigned along a north-south axis.

They conclude that, ultimately, three major north-south regional blocs will emerge: a U.S./American bloc, a European/African bloc, and an Asian bloc. They reason that the world is essentially moving towards the formation of a "U.S. of Europe," a "U.S. of Asia," and a "U.S. of the Americas" to collectively dominate the world economy. In Sheth's and Sisodia's analysis, instead of the world being flattened, the world is becoming tripolar. Going forward, each trade bloc will operate as a kind of super-country or trade-state, permitting the free flow of products, people, money, information, education and culture across all internal borders. This broader form of integration is in stark contrast to current means of creating trading blocks such as NAFTA that deal mostly with tariffs and deregulating transnational corporations. While these broad entities will never quite take the form of today's nation-states, they will come close. It's especially important for those who continue to think of America as the world's only economic superpower to recognize that, by 2050, China, alone, is forecast to have a GDP twice as large as the United States. The geoeconomic realignment has begun, and it won't be dominated by a single superpower.

In each bloc, growth is likely to be created by the economic coalition and integration of one advanced and one large emerging economy. While the developed economies of the U.S. and Germany will lead their coalitions, Sheth and Sisodia predict that China will lead Japan and South Korea. It must be emphasized, however, that the goal of this new pattern of trade is not to overrun the developing world and extract its resources in the way that corporate globalization has done until now, with its transnational corporations in the driver's seat, setting the rules of the WTO, World Bank and IMF.

Sheth and Sisodia believe that for economic progress to continue, the world needs both growth and prosperity. They note that most developed countries have high prosperity but low growth, while many developing nations have high growth but low prosperity. Thus, the surest and fastest way to benefit the largest number of people is to create true synergy by speeding integration between countries from both categories. Developed nations have high-tech know-how and infrastructure expertise. The developing world has people, youth, resources, and markets with great potential for rapid expansion. A thoughtfully planned and executed program of economic cooperation between the two worlds can result in great stability and prosperity for both.

The necessity of economic growth will force each member of this new geoeconomic triad to seek out trading partners in the developing world. The EU, which is already expanding to include Eastern European countries and Russia, will leverage its traditional ties to Africa and the Middle East and integrate them into the bloc. Implementation of the Free Trade Agreement of the Americas (FTAA) will bring Central and South America into alignment with the U.S., Canada, and Mexico. And, in Asia, Japan is already linking its economy with China, South Korea, and the ten nations in the Association of Southeast Asian Nations (ASEAN) bloc.

Sheth and Sisodia argue that the old colonial model is dead, as is the Cold War model of offering assistance to developing nations in order to gain military and ideological advantage. Even the more recent paradigm—the search for and exploitation of cheap labor—is also outmoded. Simply treating developing nations as low-wage production centers will not enhance the global competitive power of any entity.

The forces driving the world toward the tripolar structure are powerful and will not be denied. However, many challenges remain for each of the three blocs while making the transition. Each trade economy, and the countries within it, will have to adopt a formal and coordinated industrial policy to ensure that economic development proceeds in a planned, systematic manner. In particular, countries must focus on maintaining a policy free of ideology; providing incentives for quality, innovation, and productivity; stimulating economic growth; and ensuring a high degree of environmental compliance.

Besides the traditional infrastructures for water, waste, and education, countries and blocs must invest in modernizing and coordinating their other essential infrastructures, which include: facilitating the movement of people and products; enabling instantaneous any time, any place information sharing; delivering reliable energy where it is needed; and collecting, managing, and investing financial resources.

Trade blocs will have to realign their trade flows within and across regions, with particular emphasis on generating growth through emerging markets. They must realign their currencies, promote more *intrabloc* trade so as to protect their domestic sectors, and encourage *interbloc* trade as a means of enhancing and maintaining global competitiveness.

The authors believe that Europe has a significant lead—primarily because it has been the prime mover behind regionalization for several decades. The Americas are vulnerable because the FTAA has not yet been signed, and U.S. companies have barely begun the process of thinking *Americas* first. Thus, they are still facing east and west towards Europe and Asia, when they should be aligned north and south. Moreover, if the Americas can successfully integrate South Asia into its bloc, it will enjoy a significant advantage over the Europeans in having access to a large and growing population.

Finally, countries in each bloc will have to rationalize their domestic industries. This will include taking steps to facilitate sector specialization and focus, remove governmental subsidies, permit industry consolidation, regionalize domestic and global markets, and promote bloc-level standards and resource mobility.

Europe's considerable lead in this arena will grow even stronger if it can remove heavy subsidies and allow more consolidation. Since the Americas are lagging in this area, it is critical that governments in the Americas bloc start thinking more regionally and encourage bloc companies to do the same. They must communicate that, while their past has been inextricably linked with Europe, and to a lesser extent, Asia, their future lies in the Americas.

In the end, Sheth and Sisodia propose that the future health and credibility of markets will be shaped, not only by technology and global forces, but also by how different regions find their own particular solutions to the key challenges of growth, prosperity, fair and just market economies, nationalism versus market-driven pragmatics, environmental compliance, and demographics. They assert that world trade will take the form of three huge economies, which like companies in an industry, will control the lion's share of the global market, as they compete, coexist, and occasionally cooperate with each other. Similar to companies in an industry, each trade economy will have its own core competencies, vulnerabilities, and distinct formula for success within the global economy. In other words, each will evolve according to its strengths, fitness, and efficiencies. Their warning of the precarious future that Western economies face if they fail to make fundamental changes in their global economic policies is a wake-up call to confront the challenges of entrenched private sectors, political gridlock, and unrealistic expectations. The days of WTO, NAFTA, IMF and other trading platforms tilted to favor transnational corporations must give way to truly integrating regional economies and redrawing the geoeconomic map. The days of America's economic superiority are numbered, and America needs a truly integrated regional economic bloc, not the rigged terms of the proposed FTAA.

Joseph Stiglitz identifies some of the major obstacles to forming the proposed Free Trade Area of the Americas, "In the long run, while particular special-interest groups may benefit from such an unfair trade treaty, America's national interests—in having stable and prosperous neighbors—are not well served. Already, the manner in which the United States is bullying the weaker countries of Central and South America into accepting its terms is generating enormous resentment. If these trade agreements do no better for them than NAFTA has done for Mexico, then both peace and prosperity in the hemisphere will be at risk."[45]

So it seems there are continuing obstacles ahead, but a tri-polar economic world could very likely evolve. Years ago, America let go of its manufacturing might, relying, instead, on its financial power as its source of geoeconomic power. But now America is the world's largest debtor nation. It seems clear that America will not continue to be *the* superpower it was when the millennium clock rolled over to the twenty-first century, but it will, no doubt, assume its place among the leaders of a tri-polar global economic system.

Remember that around the time that engineering graduates peaked in the U.S. in 1983, China was just starting its "Four Modernizations," a movement to promote four key sectors of the economy: science and technology; agriculture; industry; and the military. If you consider that last item, geoeconomic power and geopolitical power may just go hand-in-hand. This raises interesting questions about who really won the Cold War, and whether Western-style democracies will dominate in the future. Remember that the classic text, *The Art of War,* is a Chinese treatise, and that the D-word rarely comes up in discussions of China's spectacular economic rise.

We do indeed live in interesting times, and the days of American superpoweredness and unipolarity certainly seem numbered. We'll say it one more time: *Globalization is the most profound reorganization of the world since the Industrial Revolution.*

9. A Paradigm Shift for America

As Thomas Paine wrote in December 1776, "These are the times that try men's souls. The summer soldier and the sunshine patriot will, in this crisis, shrink from the service of their country; but he that stands it now, deserves the love and thanks of man and woman. Tyranny, like hell, is not easily conquered; yet we have this consolation with us, that the harder the conflict, the more glorious the triumph."

Today's politicians and policymakers still work from a globalization mindset largely in place since the end of WWII. Few have updated their thinking around the assumptions underpinning Ricardian theories where economies of scale and the free flow of labor and capital were not part of the equation of comparative advantage. We find ourselves trying to solve today's problems with solutions that largely created the problems inherent in twenty-first century globalization. The time has come for a paradigm shift, for the world has changed.

Whatever the answers, we all need to understand far better the forces of twenty-first century globalization. America leads today, but the foundations of its leadership were forged out of the aftermath of WWI when America was the only fighter left still standing. Turning to Wikipedia for a quick recap, "The U.S. held a majority of investment capital, manufacturing production and exports. In 1945, the U.S. produced half the world's coal, two-thirds of the oil, and more than half of the electricity. The U.S. was able to produce great quantities of ships, airplanes, vehicles, armaments, machine tools, and chemicals. The U.S. also held 80% of gold reserves and had not only a powerful army but also the atomic bomb.

"As the world's greatest industrial power and one of the few nations unravaged by the war, the U.S. stood to gain more than any other country from the opening of the entire world to unfettered trade. The U.S. would have a global market for its exports, and it would have unrestricted access to vital raw materials.

"The U.S. was not only able, it was also willing to assume this leadership role. Although the U.S. had more gold, more manufacturing capacity and more military power than the rest of the world put together, U.S. capitalism could not survive without markets and allies. William Clayton, the assistant secretary of state for economic affairs, was among myriad U.S. policymakers who summed up this point: 'We need markets – big markets – around the world in which to buy and sell.'

"The 1944 Bretton Woods Conference established and set forth the rules of the International Monetary Fund (IMF) and the International Bank for Reconstruction and Development (IBRD), now the World Bank, and provided for a system of fixed exchange rates. The rules further sought to encourage an open system by committing members to the convertibility of their respective currencies into other currencies and to free trade.

"The chief features of the Bretton Woods system were an obligation for each country to adopt a monetary policy that maintained the exchange rate of its currency within a fixed value – plus or minus one percent – in terms of gold; and the ability of the IMF to bridge temporary imbalances of payments. In the face of increasing strain, the system collapsed in 1971, following the United States' suspension of convertibility from dollars to gold. Until the early 1970s, the Bretton Woods system was effective in controlling conflict and in achieving the common goals of the leading states that had created it, especially the United States. Today, the World Bank and the IMF continue, but their role has changed in many ways, although still greatly influenced by special interests in the United States."

But now it is time to fast-forward to today and the decline of U.S. hegemony. The U.S. is no longer the dominant economic power it had been for almost six decades. As Clyde Prestowitz wrote, "Maintaining a unipolar, hegemonic leadership is out of the question. It is no longer possible nor desirable for the long-term welfare of Americans. But there is much America can and should do to mitigate the impact of wage competition, maintain the promise of opportunity at the heart of the American Dream, provide for a continually rising standard of living more equitably distributed, and continue to influence the course of global affairs.

"The first step is to recognize that there is a problem. America needs to realize that many of the assumptions guiding its economic policy are at odds with the realities of today's global economy. Its performance in a broad range of areas—including savings, education, energy and water conservation, critical infrastructure, R&D investment, and workforce upskilling—is far below the standard of many other nations. America needs to understand that its refusal to have a broad competitiveness policy is, in fact, a policy. And it gives leading U.S. CEOs no choice but to play into the strategies of other countries. This policy, according to its proponents, leaves decisions to the unseen hand of the market. Actually, however, it leaves them to highly visible hands of lobbyists and foreign policy makers. It is a policy that ultimately leads to impoverishment"[46]

The time has come for an American competitiveness strategy and policy—a paradigm shift in our thinking that correlates to the realities of twenty-first century globalization. Such shift in mindset must include recommendations from some of the thought leaders on globalization. Here's a sampling:

1. Establishing a Federal Competitiveness cabinet position;
2. Providing universal health care;
3. Establishing a viable wage for all;
4. Providing education subsidies, not farm subsidies;
5. Providing world-wide education via the Internet;
6. Reducing the Federal deficit;
7. Fostering increased savings, e.g., with automatic 401K plans;
8. Reducing U.S. consumption and increasing it in Asia;
9. Ending the dollar hegemony at a new Bretton Woods-style conference;
10. Energizing energy efficiency;
11. Upgrading the U.S.' infrastructure, e.g., water, telecommunications networks, rail, etc.;
12. Having government govern corporations versus the reverse as it is today;
13. Establishing true economic unions, not asymmetric trade agreements;
14. Establishing tripolar trading blocs, not American unipolar hegemony;
15. Reforming and strengthening the IMF, World Bank, and WTO to incorporate "fair" trade;
16. Separating public goods (the commons) from private goods;
17. Developing smart, gas-sipping cars and alternative fuels for them;
18. Rethinking and reorganizing America's sprawling suburbs;
19. Revising the Tax Code, e.g., consumption and value added taxes;
20. Globalizing health care, e.g., being able to spend Medicare dollars overseas;

21. Attracting and keeping foreign talent; and
22. Developing a U.S.-China energy/ecology/technology project to help protect the planet.

This book would be hundreds more pages in length if we expounded on these strategies and their rationales. So we turn that task over to our essential readings below, where you'll find discussions and insights by Stiglitz, Prestowitz, Fingar, Sheth, Sisodia and others.

The End of the Beginning

As we come to the end of this book, we hope it is just the beginning of your interest in this vital subject of globalization. We hope our analysis of Thomas Friedman's book, *The World is Flat*, has provided you with a second take on the monumental subject of globalization. We trust that you, like us, will want to pursue this subject, for globalization affects all our lives and will be of even greater significance to our children and grandchildren.

To continue your journey, we have prepared a shortlist of suggested readings for further exploration:

Exteme Competition, by Peter Fingar, begins where *The World is Flat,* leaves off, but spares readers from Friedman's grandiloquent prose, and offers 13 concrete suggestions for action. It looks at globalization from an American perspective, and sounds a penetrating wake-up call to governments, companies, and individuals alike. It's designed as a briefing that can be read in one sitting.

Renowned trade expert Clyde V. Prestowitz takes a sobering look at economic trends and finds the United States suffering decline under globalization. While this former Reagan official's message is a frightening one, you'll have a tough time putting it down because of his lucid and cogent insights about where the world is going and why. This is a must-read for anyone who wants to stay ahead of the globalization curve.

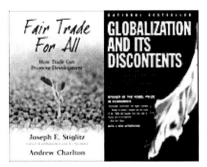

Columbia University Professor, Joseph Stiglitz is Winner of the Nobel Prize in economics and former Vice President and Chief Economist at the World Bank. You simply cannot fully understand globalization without reading Stiglitz's books.

If you ever wondered what all the massive demonstrations and riots were about at the World Trade Organization meeting in Seattle in 1999, this book will reveal why. It offers compelling alternatives to "corporate" globalization thus far, and features chapters on the global balance of power, new international sructures, corporate-government structures today, and the media.

This book argues that regionalization, characterized by extensive North-South integration between developed and developing nations, will replace the much celebrated globalization. Sheth and Sisodia argue that these evolving, strategic partnerships will involve free trade, monetary union, cross-border infrastructure investments, regional development agencies, and conflict resolution mechanisms.

We wish you great success in your globalization journey ahead.

For additional readings, and to join in on our blog visit
www.mkpress.com/flat

References

[1] http://query.nytimes.com/gst/fullpage.html?res=9D07E6DB1731F932A3 5756C0A9639C8B63

[2] http://www.boston.com/ae/books/articles/2005/04/03/on_the_level/

[3] http://www.spectator.co.uk/books.php?id=2857

[4] http://tinyurl.com/ohcy6

[5] Amitabh Pal, "The pundit and the money tree," *The Progressive,* July, 2005

[6] http://www.vuw.ac.nz/pols/Journals/Antepodium/articles/hoogvelt-1997.aspx

[7] http://www.slate.com/id/2116899/

[8] http://nypress.com/print.cfm?content_id=12841

[9] http://www.imfsite.org/operations/sick.html

[10] Joseph Stiglitz, "The ruin of Russia," *The Guardian,* April 9, 2003.

[11] http://www.washingtonpost.com/wp-dyn/articles/A23725-2004Nov30.html

[12] http://en.wikipedia.org/wiki/Business_process_management

[13] http://money.cnn.com/services/tickerheadlines/for5/200605311814DOWJONESDJONLINE001157_FORTUNE5.htm

[14] Waite, Steve, "Digitization GE Style," *Canadian Hedge Watch Newsletter,* May 7, 2001.

[15] Quoted in Extreme Competition, Meghan-Kiffer Press, 2006.

[16] http://www.chiefexecutive.net/depts/technology/197a.htm

[17] Lawrence Lessig and Robert W. McChesney, "No Tolls on The Internet," *The Washington Post,* June 8, 2006.

[18] http://www.itpaa.org/modules.php?name=News&file=article&sid=1705

[19] Fingar, Peter, *Extreme Competition: Innovation and the Great 21ˢᵗ Century Business Reformation,* Meghan-Kiffer Press, 2006.

[20] http://www.heifer.org/site/c.edJRKQNiFiG/b.1459289/

[21] Gray, John, "he World is Round," *New York Review of Books,* Volume 52, Number 13 (August 11 2005)

[22] http://www.counterpunch.org/cockburn06102005.html

[23] http://hrw.org/reports/2005/china0405/3.htm#_Toc100128606

[24] http://www.appleinsider.com/article.php?id=1799

[25] *New York Times Magazine,* March 28, 1999

[26] http://enjoyment.independent.co.uk/books/reviews/article334756.ece

[27] http://www.heifer.org/site/c.edJRKQNiFiG/b.1459289

[28] http://www.thenation.com/doc/20010528/forum/2

[29] http://billnelson.senate.gov/news/details.cfm?id=257058&

[30] http://www.theglobalist.com/StoryId.aspx?StoryId=4964

[31] http://www.gregpalast.com/detail.cfm?artid=447&row=0

[32] Phillips, Kevin, *American Theocracy,* Viking, 2006.

33 http://www.washingtonpost.com/ac2/wp-dyn/A38725-2005Apr8?language=printer

34 Taylor Loyal, "Don't Leave College Without It," MotherJones.com, March 2002

35 http://www.thenation.com/doc/20060417/forum/2

36 http://bigpicture.typepad.com/comments/2005/04/wages_and_consu.html

37 http://bigpicture.typepad.com/comments/2005/04/wages_and_consu.html

38 http://www.truthout.org/docs_04/112804K.shtml

39 http://bernie.house.gov/statements/20040227132145.asp

40 http://www.harvard-magazine.com/on-line/010682.html

41 http://www.reclaimthecommons.net/article.php?id=259

42 http://www.uncwil.edu/smartgrowth/activities/worksheet-letter.html

43 http://www.mindfully.org/Sustainability/Hawken-Resource-Waste.htm

44 http://www.navdanya.org/articles/end-poverty.htm

45 Stiglitz, Joseph E., "The Broken Promise of NAFTA," *New York Times,* January 6, 2004.

46 Prestowitz, Clyde, *Three Billion New Capitalists*, Basic Books, 2005.

Index

About the Authors

RONALD ARONICA is a business analyst and consultant to business and governmental organizations. In his writings, including the book, *The Death of 'e' and the Birth of the Real New Economy*, he uses his more than thirty years experience to help readers separate hype from reality.

MTETWA "TET" RAMDOO is an independent business research analyst. She focuses on the impact of globalization on various industries, and the overall impact of globalization on business and social transformation.

Companion Book ...
www.mkpress.com/extreme

"This is the definitive guide to business success in the new age of total global competition." —Clyde Prestowitz